MIN SETS

Change Your
PERCEPTIONS, Create
New **PERSPECTIVES** and
Cultivate Greater **CLARITY**

MINDSETS

Mike George
Reveals the Secrets of
CLEAR THINKING

Change Your
PERCEPTIONS, Create
New **PERSPECTIVES** and
Cultivate Greater **CLARITY**

GAVISUS
media

MINDSETS

Change Your PERCEPTIONS, Create New
PERSPECTIVES and Cultivate Greater CLARITY

Mike George
Text Copyright Mike George 2015

Print Edition ISBN: 978-0-9576673-7-2
Also available as an E-Book

First published by Gavisus Media 2015
805 Bayswater Tower
Al Abraj Street
PO Box 211965 Business Bay Dubai, UAE
Email: gavisusmedia@gmail.com

The moral rights of the author have been asserted.
Cover Design: Charlotte Mouncey - www.bookstyle.co.uk

The information given in this book should not be treated as a substitute
for professional medical advice; always consult a medical practitioner. Any
use of information in this book is at the reader's discretion and risk. Neither
the author nor the publisher can be held responsible for any loss, claim or
damage arising out of use, or misuse, or the suggestions made
or the failure to take medical advice

Other Books by Mike George

BEING Your Self
SEEing and KNOWing What's IN the Way IS the Way!

The Immune System of the SOUL
How to Free Your Self from ALL Forms of Dis - ease

The 7 Myths About LOVE...Actually!
The Journey from Your HEAD to the HEART of Your SOUL

Don't Get MAD Get Wise
Why no one ever makes you angry...ever!

The 7 AHA!s of Highly Enlightened Souls
How to Free YOUR Self from ALL Forms of Stress

Learn to Find Inner Peace
Manage your anxieties, think well, feel well.

Learn to Relax
Ease tension, conquer stress and free the self

In the Light of Meditation
A guide to meditation and spiritual development

1001 Ways to Relax
Beat stress and find perfect calm, anywhere, anytime!

1001 Meditations
Discover peace of mind

Dedication

To those who often hear themselves privately thinking
'I can't' or 'I am not able' or 'I don't know...'.
Always remember to add one word...
YET!

YET opens the space between here and there, between
now and the moment when you can,
when you do, when you know.

But before you try to fill that space with the search for the magic
formula, with the momorization of more information, with the
mastery of technique, with the endevour of learning,
remind your self of this:

Life happens not from outside in but from inside out.
Everything from love to wisdom, from confidence to happiness,
from fullfilment to friendship, happens naturally when your
mindset is shaped not by the 'beliefs' that others have told you
but when you see and realize what is 'true' for your self.

Here is a set of signposts that point to what you already
know, but have inconveniently forgotten!

Don't 'believe' a word that you read!
Better to use the insights and ideas to reflect
and re-awaken within you what is 'true' for you!

May you remember with ease
and make YET redundant!

CONTENTS

Change Your
PERCEPTIONS

Your perception is your reality. As you perceive so you create. As you create so you will project. As we project together so we co-create the world... together! So it is that the 'outer' is simply a manifestation of the 'inner'. According to your perception of the state of the world so you will also 'see' the current state of your being, which is you!

Create New
PERSPECTIVES

As is your 'point of view' so will be your unique perspective. As you change your 'point of viewing' so your perspective will shift. So it is that in the universe of conversation no one perspective is right or wrong, absolutely true or absolutely untrue. But some perspectives will always be more 'accurate' than others! Accuracy is the foundation of a life well lived. Pursue accuracy!

Cultivate Greater
CLARITY

Whatever you are attached to or dependent on will always cloud your vision and skew your decisions. Only when you are free in your being can you 'see' clearly and 'discern' accurately. Only then will your mind reflect that clarity and your thoughts start to give form to that clarity.

Clear thinking is almost no thinking compared to the mental chaos and confusion within the mind of an unfree being! Pursue real freedom!

What's in YOUR Mindset?

Your MINDSET will dictate your decisions today and shape your destiny tomorrow. Your MINDSET will define the quantity and the quality of all your relationships. Your thoughts and feelings at any given moment will not be the product of other people's behavior or where you are in the world or what is going on in the world - you will think and feel entirely according to your own MINDSET!

A MINDSET is essentially a belief or belief system. As we filter everything through our beliefs we create **perceptions** and **thoughts**, which then shape your decisions, feelings and behaviors. We form our MINDSETS at three levels as we create and sustain beliefs about the world, about others and about our self.

Your MINDSETS about the World

For example, if you 'believe' the world is a dark and dangerous place

Beliefs 'set' the mind as they shape perception and perspective! However most of our beliefs do not produce clarity of vision or accuracy of thought, more often they are the fog that stops us from seeing reality!

you will tend to perceive/interpret events mostly as a threat, generate fear in the form of anxiety, create a habit of becoming defensive or aggressive, and generally live an unhappy and insecure life. However if you 'believe' the world is an adventure playground then you will perceive situations and circumstances as an opportunity to play. You will exercise and focus your creative abilities proactively, and generally be able to maintain a stable and happy state of mind.

Your MINDSETS about Other People

If you 'believe', as Jean Paul Sartre once suggested, that 'hell is other people', (or another person!) then you will perceive many if not most of your relationships as having to be tolerated and suffered. Your energy around people will tend to be dark and dispiriting, and you will frequently generate feelings of resentment and foreboding. If, on the other hand, you believe all relationship is a dynamic process of being enriched and enriching others, that every relationship is an opportunity to 'be creative', you will enthusiastically engage with almost all those that you connect with.

Your MINDSETS about... You!

If you 'believe' you are not worthy and cannot change your personality or learn new skills or develop new talents, there is a good chance you will start to 'perceive' your life as a pointless waste of time and energy. Hopelessness and helplessness will likely be frequent visitors as you give up easily on any endeavors that require significant enthusiasm to follow through.

Whereas, if you 'believe' there is nothing you cannot learn and do, that you can change your personality and create many new attributes within your character, you will enthusiastically find ways to improve, enhance, develop, learn, unlearn and grow your... self!

Each one of us 'can know' the MINDSETS that we have created and carry within our consciousness. But it seems few of us will make that kind of 'inner enquiry'. Few reflect deeply enough to see and understand the beliefs that make up the MINDSETS that may be sabotaging their life. This is why so few people actually change the quality of their life, why so few enhance their personal capacities, why so few stretch themselves to find new ways to be alive and 'do life'.

Too Entrenched

Many approaches to training, personal development and coaching don't work to any significant depth because old habits, based on old MINDSETS, based on inaccurate beliefs, are too entrenched within consciousness. Attitudes and behavior, and the consequent outcomes, only change when your MINDSET changes. This means becoming aware of the beliefs that you have assimilated and created, then challenging those beliefs and consciously changing them through a process of realization i.e. realizing which beliefs are the basis of your illusions and delusions and which ones are just not 'true'!

There are two ways to induce the kind of realizations that will alter your beliefs and belief systems – meditation and contemplation. Meditation gives you access to the deeper states of consciousness where you will always find your peace, which in turn allows you to generate a deeper, truer 'insight'. From meditation comes the AHA moments of self-realization. You realize exactly which old beliefs are just that, 'old beliefs', and why many of them are just not true!

The other practise, ideally cultivated in parallel to some kind of meditation practise, is 'contemplation'. This means exploring different, wiser and clearer perceptions of how

The deepest and most influential beliefs that we all hold and that take us all 'off track', are beliefs about our self! At this level NO beliefs are true! There are no methods or techniques to achieve this reawakening of the awareness of the true, authentic and real self - the self that is prior to all learned beliefs. Learning is therefore almost irrelevant and 'unlearning' is the only way to 'induce' self-realization and restore clarity, which then naturally empowers the individual, from inside out, to make significant changes to their attitudes and behaviors!

the world works, how to make relationships work and why 'you' are not thinking and feeling very well within your self! By contemplating the insights and wisdom of others, alongside your own personal insperiences, you allow your self to rediscover the deeper truths that already exist within your consciousness, within YOU!

Only You Can Do it!

The purpose of this book is to offer you a series of reflections that may help you to see from a different angle, see with greater accuracy and clarity, realize the deeper truths that may allow you to live with greater freedom, happiness and power. No one can alter your MINDSET. No one can make you change your beliefs. No one can create your decisions for you. No one can alter your attitude or your behavior.

You already know all that you need to know in order to change and realize your full potential. All you need to do is 'unlearn' what is in the way, which is usually what you 'believe' you know!

It seems obvious to say that, but most of us are running around with the 'belief' that we can change others beliefs, attitudes and behaviors, and therefore that others can change ours. But it's just not 'true'. We are each 100% responsible for everything that occurs within our consciousness. And everything we think, feel and do begins within our consciousness, within our self.

But you can be 'influenced'. You can be assisted, guided, coached! And you can 'influence' others. But influence is not control!

For the last ten years the regular CLEAR THINKING essays and articles have been circulating monthly around the world to people deeply interested in cultivating greater clarity about the MINDSETS that are required to live their day-to-day life with less stress and greater joy.

Being deeply and profoundly interested in the meaning of life and how to fully live this life, I have spent the last 33 years 'researching' inside and out. One way that I create, sustain and increase clarity for my self is to write and share what I am seeing and realizing. Yes I have been guided by the many wise words of others, by the 'insperiences' of others, by both easy and difficult interactions with others, but mostly I share what has occurred within me as a result of my own practises of meditation, contemplation and application.

One of the first pieces of advice that I usually give to anyone I am coaching is to write something every day about what is going on within you. As that old saying reminds us, "How do I know what I know until I hear what I have to say". We all have a deep font of wisdom at the heart of our being. We already know what is real and unreal, what is true and what is false, what is accurate and inaccurate – it's just that we forget HOW to look within our self, see clearly and then accurately interpret what we find within, and thereby recognize what is true and real.

The purpose of this book, a selection of some of the clearest CLEAR THINKING essays, is to provide you with some signposts on both where and how to look, how to be more aware of what is occurring within you, alongside some different interpretations of what is really happening in the world of our relationships. Altogether they are intended to provide you with some clues and signals on how to challenge your own beliefs, alter your own perceptions and reshape your perspectives, so that greater clarity may prevail as you 'decide' how to live your life. As you do this inner work you will gradually notice both natural and significant shifts in your MINDSETS.

And when your MINDSET changes, it changes almost everything.

As always if something is not clear feel free to make contact at mike@relax7.com

Have YOU Found
True 'For Giveness'?

There is a huge difference between a hurt body and hurt feelings. Someone or some thing can cause you to feel physical pain but no one can cause you to suffer emotionally... if you so decide! However, it seems that few us learn to make the clear distinction between physical pain and emotional suffering. As the old saying goes *pain is compulsory but suffering is optional*. Unless it's chronic, then 'physical pain' is usually a one-time event before it subsides. But 'emotional suffering' tends to linger longer.

Sticks and Stones

Our feelings usually 'hurt' following something someone says about us, to us, or behaves badly towards us. Those feelings can remain for a long time, depending on how much we repeat the experience in our own minds. And yet, if we cast our mind back to the school playground we may remember singing, "Sticks and stones may break my bones but names can never hurt me". We would call each other horrible names and mock each other mercilessly and yet, the next moment, we would play on as if nothing had been said. Unfortunately, as we grow up, we tend to become increasingly sensitive to what other people say to us and about us. Suddenly we start taking things personally and we are easily offended. Why? We create an ego.

As we grow we develop our ego, which is essentially an image of ourselves that we create in our own minds. We become attached to that image and it becomes our subtle identity. If people say or do anything that contradicts that image we become offended and create what we call 'hurt feelings' or, more accurately, feelings of hurt. We inflict emotional suffering upon our self.

From childhood to adulthood we gradually become more sensitive, and no one teaches us the basic principle that can start to set us free of our own self-created suffering. It sounds something like this: "No one can hurt me, but I can use you to hurt my self".

Clear Distinction

We are, of course, talking about our emotions and not our body. When someone hurts your body they don't hurt you, they hurt your body. You feel the physical pain as the body sends the appropriate signals to the brain. But the hurt feelings i.e. 'emotional suffering', is always a choice. We can choose to instantly forget the physical pain and it's cause if we want, or we can keep remembering it and keep generating anger and/or resentment towards the person who caused the physical pain. It's a choice, but only if we can see the choice. And it seems many can't, simply because no one teaches us to be aware of the emotions that we create and feel. No one teaches us to make the distinction between physical pain and emotional suffering. Even fewer of us learn that we are entirely responsible for our emotional state at all times. Realizing that you are the creator of your feelings (the emotions that you feel) and that you can therefore choose your feelings is one of the most significant steps in re-empowering your self and being the master of your own life.

For most of us there are seven frequent occurrences, following which we tend to generate emotional suffering (what we call hurt feelings). These are moments when people insult us, gossip about us, ignore us, reject us, betray us, deceive us or let us down. These are the behaviors that may 'trigger' our belief that we have been hurt, but they never actually 'cause' our hurt feelings. Here is why.

You REJECTED me!

We feel rejected when we interpret others attitudes and behavior towards us as non-accepting. If it happens often enough we will start looking for evidence of rejection almost as soon as we meet someone. The belief that we are 'rejectable', that for some reason we are not worthy of others acceptance, has set in. If it pains us emotionally, if we feel hurt by others apparent rejection, it means we are coming to the relationship in a state of neediness. It's the need to be accepted and approved by the other which underlies any hurt feelings. It's this neediness that usually sits under any insecurity that we may feel in any relationship. If we can free our self from needing to acquire the acceptance and approval of others we would probably never 'decide' to feel hurt by their behavior towards us even if it was overtly rejecting. Not so easy in a world where most of us are taught to build our sense of self on how others see us and act towards us.

You IGNORED me!

Sometimes it seems there is nothing worse than being ignored by another. Even worse if it's by a group of 'others'! At least in rejection there is some engagement, some acknowledgment of our presence and existence! Can we live without the acknowledgement of another? Can we survive being ignored? Well we usually do. But it's emotionally painful because we are dependent on others acknowledgement to give us the feeling that we exist and that we are of value. Perhaps the only way free of yet another form of neediness is to affirm our own existence and to find ways to make our self of value to 'different others'. Being of value to others is the context in which we grow our awareness of our own value, our own worth. And when we 'know' our value, which is also one of the deepest foundations of self-confidence, our neediness dissolves. Then, if someone ignores us, it's OK! We know our value! Besides, who knows why 'they' do what they do, it's their choice! It may just be an expression of their belief in their own lack of self-value!

You DECEIVED me!

It's hard to overcome the feeling of hurtfulness when you know someone has lied to you, when you know you've been 'had', when you believe you've been deceived. We expect others, especially those close to us, to be honest and open and well... straight! So we are not only surprised when there is deception, we take it personally, and start to feel hurt by the other.

We then upset our self when they behave in ways that we don't expect.

Sometimes it's a hurt that we will hold on to for many years. But it's not the others deviousness that hurts us, it's our expectation of them. It's our sense of our self as someone who is worthy of 'their' best behavior, of their honesty, of their respect, that is the underlying cause of our feeling offended. We then upset our self when they behave in ways that we don't expect, in ways that do not acknowledge and affirm the image we have of our self i.e. as someone deserving of the honesty, respect and openness of others.

The only way to free our self from our hurt is to seek to understand them. When we find out why they seem to have deceived us we usually find it's nothing to do 'with me' and more to do with a flaw in their character, a fear of revealing something, an avoidance of being exposed, a strategy to hide something from us. We will likely find they are, in some way, fear full! Only our understanding of the other can give us the internal impetus to transform our hurt and condemnation into understanding and compassion.

Ultimately the deepest way to be free of what we call 'hurt feelings', in almost all such instances, is to drop your expectations of the other. But if that's a bridge too far then perhaps, to begin with, you can separate your happiness from having your expectations met. Can you have an expectation free day? Can you put aside all expectations of the other, and still be content within your self?

You are spreading GOSSIP about me!

We live in the age of the gossip. The media has spawned its many social offspring and they love to keep us busy! Social media gives us access to others people's lives and an opportunity to interpret, comment and tell stories about other peoples activities. It gives us the power to build a reputation and project that reputation to hundreds of thousands of people almost instantly. That's when we become 'reputation dependent'! We want others to see and think of us in a certain way, usually as a good person (minimum) and perhaps also as a great person (maximum!) if not a beautiful person! We then become dependent on others affirmation of our goodness, acknowledgement of our beauty, if not our greatness!

We want to be recognized and we become dependent on others for how we see our self and feel about our self. It's no surprise we become super sensitive to what others are saying about us. Or indeed NOT saying about us! And it's even less of a surprise when we become easily hurt by the slightest slur on our character. Sometimes simply the absence of admiration (how many 'likes' did I receive today?) is enough to tip us into feeling ever so slightly... hurt!

Sometimes we encounter someone who has no concern for what others think of him or her whatsoever. Yet they are still warm and sensitive people to be with. We may say they have a thick skin. Deep down however we probably appreciate, respect and even admire their ability to stay unfazed by the judgments, stories and even slander that others may spread about them. They seem to be free on the inside. They are not dependent on others for how they see and feel about themselves. They are internally free spirits!

You LET ME DOWN!

"You let me down. I'm so disappointed in you". Both statements are code for 'you made me suffer'! It's one of the most prevalent illusions of modern society. Often, it's also the first line in the process of 'emotional blackmail! These exchanges usually start somewhere in childhood, in the relationship between parent and child. In those moments we learn that we are responsible for others feelings and therefore others are responsible for our feelings. They are fatal lessons. They will guarantee a lifetime of unhappiness born of a dependency on others for what we feel within our self. The only way free is to realize that no one is responsible for what you feel; no one ever lets you down! You let your self down. And 'down' usually means you bring your self 'down' from a happy or contented state to a sad or agitated state...even when 'they' are just five minutes late!

Sometimes it's the smallest thing that seems to trigger your 'down'. Imagine a life where, regardless of what others do or what anyone else says, you cannot be 'let down'. Can you smell the freedom, the stability, the contentment within your self and, at the same time, you would have consistent ability to 'be there' for others regardless of what they do, of how 'late' or 'remiss' they may be. Is that not what we sometimes call unconditional love? Is that not the mark of a real leader?

The only way to feel free is to realize that no one is responsible for what you feel; no one ever lets YOU down!

You INSULTED me!

"I was so offended when they said that to me. It was such an insult when they said that to you. I am not only going to be personally offended but I'm also going to be offended on your behalf!" Well perhaps we don't say exactly that, but we do become indignant and create the feeling of being insulted even when others are insulted and it wasn't directed at us. It's as if we identify with their suffering and join in, ensuring that we suffer with them. Some people will remember an insult for the rest of their lives and not realize the memory is as good as the best prison cell! They lock themselves up in the memory of the images and feelings of their moment of emotional pain. Then, perhaps one day, they may see that it wasn't them that was insulted it was just an image they have of themselves that was in contradiction to what was said. They may realize that the 'self', the 'I' that says 'I am', has no image. The 'self' creates images in the mind, but has no image of itself! This takes us into spiritual territory, which is why it's probably the deepest level of freedom that a human being can 'realize'. And when we do live from this free, inner space, it just doesn't matter what anyone says to us, it will have no effect. And we certainly won't be saying, "You just hurt my feelings'. Besides anyone throwing insults around is also suffering inside. So compassion towards them not only ensures we don't lose the emotional plot, it may also be a gift for them!

You BETRAYED me!

"But you promised. You promised you wouldn't say anything. You said you wouldn't tell!" We all view the breaking of a promise as a betrayal. The worst seems to be the transfer of a 'promised exclusive intimacy' from one to another. Otherwise known as an affair! The hurt feelings go deep and often turn out to be expensive! What started out as love can end as a hate filled resentment. The emotional wounds may last a lifetime. But wait a minute! Why all the weeping and wailing? Why the indescribable emotional pain and everlasting misery? Could it just be expectation again? Could it just be dependency on another to bolster our own ego... again?

Could it be that we didn't realize that trusting another and then expecting that trust to be upheld, fulfilled, respected and reciprocated was just our 'mistake'? Who knows what makes someone betray or break a trust. There could be a thousand reasons ranging from their fears to their weaknesses. But as long as we 'expect', as long as we 'depend', as long as we 'believe' the other will never betray us, then we can also pretty much guarantee that one day we are going to feel hurt, let down, devastated, for a few moments or for a very long time. Unless! Unless we realize the emotional hurt is our responsibility. Unless we realize we have a choice. Not an easy choice to see in such moments for sure. But we don't have to suffer. People break promises. People betray! People fail to meet expectations. That's a reality on planet earth! Why are we arguing with reality?

Paradoxically, or perhaps weirdly, in the middle of such suffering we may even have the thought, "What did I do to make them betray me?" As we turn the emotional gun on our self. Crazy! So crazy it's almost pure comedy! But it doesn't feel like it at the time.

And so... the result of understanding what's really going on during and after all these reasons to 'feel hurt' is seeing that it's not 'them' that is hurting my feelings, it's me that is generating the emotional

"Believing that we can and do need to forgive the other can be slightly irrelevant - it only affirms our self-image as a victim!"

suffering. It's usually a mix of sadness and anger. That's why, at an emotional level, believing that we can and do need to forgive the other is slightly irrelevant. It only affirms our self-image as a victim. And that's the best invitation for it to happen again. There is in fact a deeper level of forgiveness that can release us from all such moments of emotional pain.

All of these scenarios have one thing in common. There is one reason why we are hurting our self emotionally in each of these seven examples. It's dependency. It's the moment when we think, "I am not getting what I WANT or they are not doing what I WANT or they are not being the way I WANT!"

In such moments we are really saying we believe, "My life is 'for getting' what I WANT. I am alive, I am here, in order to GET something". But that's not quite the purpose of life. That's not quite how life is designed to be lived. The sages and the saints have reminded us for eons that the primary purpose of live is not to GET! We don't come here to GET something, we come here to GIVE.

To GIVE of our Self.

As soon as you realize, "My life is FOR GIVING," you discover the true meaning of forgiveness, for giving! When you stop depending and expecting, which are just 'wanting' in disguise, it will be almost impossible to be emotionally hurt. Then, if and when you realize the truth that you are never hurt emotionally by anyone, the idea of forgiveness becomes irrelevant.

So, when someone stands on your foot on the train there is a moment of truth in action, a moment when you are being tested. Will you forgive and forget their clumsiness for the moment of your pain and get on with your life. Or will you fume with an indignant anger and suffer for the rest of your journey? Or will you take complete responsibility for placing your foot there in the first place?

Answers on a postcard to...

Question:
Which of the seven reasons do you experience as your most frequent 'excuse' to create emotional suffering in your life?

Reflection:
On the last two occasions you felt emotionally hurt what is it that you want/wanted from the other that they did not give you/be for you?

Action:
Choose to give something of your self to the person whom you previously thought was the cause of your hurt feelings (but now you know they were just a trigger!) and notice how this 'giving' heals your hurt.

Are YOU Playing the Game?

Across the land, on any given day, there are hundreds of people sitting in learning environments called workshops, seminars, courses and classes. As part of their learning process some will participate in 'role playing' exercises. Many will be extremely uncomfortable attempting to play a role, which they think is totally alien to them. And yet life itself is designed to give us all the opportunity to 'role play'. Some would say that's all we do from the day we arrive 'on stage' to the day we exit stage left!

Shakespeare pointed the way when he said something like, "All the world is a stage and all men and women merely players, with many parts to play". Have you ever noticed each day is filled with many scenes – the scene of the office, the scene of the kitchen, the scene of the church, the scene of the tennis court, the scene of the seminar etc. Every scene is an invitation and an opportunity to play a different role. If we do not create and play the appropriate role we will likely find the scene both mentally and emotionally difficult.

Yet, when we do recognize this opportunity it begs the question how many roles can we play in our lives? The obvious answer is as many as we want! In fact, not only do we get to **play** as many roles as we want, we also get to **create** each role. With this realization life suddenly becomes a truly playful and creative adventure. But what do we tend to do? We tend to take it all far too seriously? We forget (if we ever remembered) that life is simply a game in which we get the chance to express our self, and in so doing, give of our self, and in so doing, know our self. This realization of our unlimited creative potential is an intrinsic possibility waiting to arise from within all human beings. But it's a realization that is often suppressed by a learned belief system, a mindset, that says 'I can't' or 'I am not good enough' of 'I am not capable' or 'I am not creative'.

"Why does life become so seriously serious so often for so many people?"

So why do we take it all so seriously? Why are we not as playful as we could be? Why do so many of us suppress our creativity? Why do we not see life as a game? Here are the seven key reasons why we tend to make the business of living a serious business!

1 You are NOT a position, you're just playing another role.

If you are a manager in an organization or a parent in a family that's not all you are in the organization or the family. Manager/parent is just a doorway to many roles. As you walk through the scenes of your average day if you see your self just as 'the manager/parent' you are less likely to see the invitations and opportunities to play many roles including leader, facilitator, teacher, counselor, coach, motivator, helper etc. If the manager or parent sees their role as a position they are likely to become rigid in outlook and attitude as they fixate on their role and seek recognition for their role.

The parent will miss the signals and cues that are calling them to play a whole range of roles such a friend, guide, teacher, advisor, coach, and playmate to their children. Parents, like managers, tend to create and 'hide in' only one role, that of 'supreme controller'! It's no wonder so many of us grow up with anything from an inferiority complex to a victim mindset, accompanied by a serious deficiency of a 'life is fun' mindset!

2 Identifying with the role.

Behind all seriousness is fear, mostly in the form of anxiety. When we identify our self *with* the role we learn to believe we *are* the role. When anything appears to threaten the role, as it must, we take it personally and become fearful, defensive or aggressive. Hence the 'seriousness' of so many people whose role is defined by the organization to which they believe they belong! We are almost trained to identify with our position, which we then perceive as 'permanent' and secure. We forget that nothing is permanent in the world, and security can never be found in that which must change! This is also why the lives of many children are less than the happiest possible when the parent sees themselves as 'the parent' around here, and therefore 'the authority' on everything... around here! Seldom are parents the experts on 'how to be creative and have fun'!

3 The habit of self-limitation – "I can't act!"

If we have learned to limit ourselves in any way, and it seems the vast majority of us have, then we will likely believe we cannot be the actor who plays 'many' roles. We will justify and disguise our self-limitation by saying things like, "It's unnatural to play many roles, you are not being authentic, you are deceiving others by not being yourself". Ultimately it's the same as "I can't paint" or "I can't write". Self-limitation becomes a dis-ease of the mind and a fixed mindset! Everyone can paint and everyone can write. Everyone can act because we are all creators of actions. Roles are simply created sets of mental and physical actions and, like anything else, can be learned, which means 'developed'. And when they are learned and developed they are not aspects of a false persona. They are simply abilities that we can all cultivate to deal creatively, and therefore effectively and more satisfyingly, with the scenes of life and our immediate relationships in those scenes.

"We forget that nothing is permanent in the world, and security can never be found in that which must change!"

4 An education to be productive and not creative.

Our education system prepares us to 'produce and consume' much more than 'create and innovate'. Consequently many of us never fully realize our creative capacity. If we do it tends to be narrowed by a particular talent. But creativity is a capacity that transcends talent. It's prior to talent. Talent is just one dimension of our multidimensional capacity to be innovative. Our capacity for 'possibility thinking' is seldom fully developed. Few of us learn how to create the appropriate thoughts, attitudes and actions for

"Life is not a game in the competitive sense but a game in the true sense – an activity filled with fun and creative opportunity."

the many possible roles we can potentially play. Perhaps this is why those who go to 'drama school' are profoundly changed and expanded by the experience. Our creativity tends to be suppressed as we are subtly streamed into a society that requires people to fill a 'position' and play only one role. Occasionally we meet someone who has broken out of their 'position' mindset. They exude a vibrant and creative energy as we quietly wonder, "How do I do that?"

5 Games have winners and losers.

When 'game' is mentioned as a possible metaphor for life some of us will automatically run away. For them 'game' means competition and that means winners and losers. The fear of losing paralyses our creativity and we shy away from full participation in life. But life is not a game in the competitive sense but a game in the truest sense – an activity filled with fun and creative opportunity. No one loses when we co-create. No one loses when we join in and innovate with others. We may fall asleep occasionally and re-ignite the old fear based winners and losers mindset. But no one loses...ultimately! If 'they' do...we all do! So deep is our belief and conditioned perception of life as 'a competition' it is often one of the hardest beliefs to challenge and perceptions to shake off.

6 Someone else is responsible.

When we still believe that life is not a creative process that comes from inside out, but something that 'happens to us' from outside in, we have still not realized our responsibility for our own life. Only when self-responsibility is fully realized will the awareness of life as a creative process begin to increase. Otherwise we project onto institutions, governments and media the responsibility for 'creating' our feelings and decisions and therefore our life. Hence the most popular dis – ease in the world is known as 'victimitis'.

7 "I don't play games!"

If you watch yourself in those more serious moments you may notice that you have developed a judgmental tendency towards others. When you interpret their motives and behaviors as political games, games of manipulation and spin, games of attempting to keep others down, games that are designed to exploit and extract your money, games that are then dressed up as normal and part of life, you can easily become disillusioned with life itself. Cynicism is just around the corner. You suppress your intuitive faith that life is essentially benevolent.

You may even start to see living as life threatening! You may even feel cursed. The very notion that life is a joyful adventure will appear to be insane. Instead, you are always on the lookout to see who might be trying to take advantage of you. From this mindset you don't even begin to realize how you may live more creatively and therefore more joyfully. The very idea of creating and playing many roles will seem irrelevant, perhaps ridiculous and maybe even distasteful. For you life has become far too serious for that. So your creative capacity is almost completely stunted and repressed. Only a radical overhaul of your beliefs and perceptions will fix this. Only a brand new mindset can release your creative potential. All complaints and criticisms, judgmentalism and projection, have to end if your creativity and playfulness are to return. Only then can joy re-appear in your heart.

Yes of course there are many who are suffering in the world, many who are apparently being taken advantage of, many who have barely enough to eat, with little or no shelter. It would seem that simply being playful and creative is not going to help them. But then why are they in those circumstances? Because sometime, somewhere in the past, someone started to take life, for whatever reason (usually fear), far too seriously. You may decide to make it one of your roles to help such people. In which case you will need to be very creative (resourceful) and very playful (light) if you are to give them the kind of help that ultimately helps them help themselves, and the kind of hope that eventually takes them beyond the need for hope at all!

That truly is what is known as a 'creative challenge'!

Question:
List all the possible roles you think you could play in the current context of your life. Then rate what you sense is your current ability to play each role well (1 is low 10 is high).

Reflection:
Why are you not as playful/creative in your relationships as you could be?

Action:
Profile the skills and abilities you need to learn to play each of the above roles well.

(PS - please don't take all these questions too seriously, play with them and see what arises in your mind and in your heart?)

Have YOU Found the Paradoxes on the Path?

Have you noticed how life, at all levels, is riddled with paradox? "Paradox" comes from two Greek words: *para* + *doksos*, meaning 'beyond the teaching' or 'beyond the opinion'. A paradox arises when we start to reconcile seeming contradictions, consciously or unconsciously. G. K. Chesterton once said, "A paradox is often a truth standing on its head to get our attention"! Paradoxes are statements containing concepts that appear contradictory but which hide a deeper truth e.g. the paradox that standing is more tiring than walking. It seems

"No surprise then that someone once said, "Through the gates of paradox you shall find the truth".

illogical to think that standing is more tiring than walking, but it's true. The deeper truth being physical energy enlivens, refreshes and renews more when it is moving than standing still.

The seeing and the realization of paradox can set us free from the constraints of what can appear to be illogical thinking. If you ever set out to find the meaning of life, the universe and everything you will likely encounter the following seven apparent paradoxes on the path!

1 The Paradox of GIVING and RECEIVING

You cannot receive unless you give

We may be aware that our relationships are defined by a dynamic of giving and receiving at a variety of levels (objects, ideas, attention, time etc.) but the inherent paradox in this dynamic is that giving is receiving and receiving is giving. In order to **receive** you have to 'give the other' the opportunity to give! In order to **give** you first have to receive the others openness to receiving!

At the spiritual level of giving and receiving this paradox takes an even deeper form. We all know, from experience, that when we give 'with love' that we feel the love that already lives within us on its way out. In essence, only by giving love can we know that love is what we have and what we are. It's not that there are two selves, but by giving love to others it's as if we are receiving it from our self. It means that as it flows from us we come to know love is what we are. Conversely, the more open we are to receiving the love of others the more we are 'giving' to them the opportunity to (receive) feel and know themselves as love.

No surprise then that someone once said, "Through the gates of paradox you shall find the truth". When we consciously seek the deeper truths in life it's more than likely we will find paradox waiting for us. It invites us to turn what seems to be logically impossible on its head!

2 The Paradox of HAVING HAPPINESS

The more you have the less content you will be

The idea of acquiring/having things is to have happiness. The search for happiness sits behind all that we want. Yet most people testify to the fact that the more external 'stuff' they have the less internal peace and contentment they experience. Acquisitions become traps for our thoughts and feelings, triggering the anxiety of insecurity (fear of loss/damage). We become slaves to what we believe we possess. Authentic happiness, whose deepest form is contentment, is not possible unless we are mentally free of the 'anxiety of insecurity'. Perhaps that's why happier people tend to have fewer acquisitions. This is not a new observation, it is not an original wisdom, but it seems to be something we need remind our self of every day if we are to be happy in a world surrounded by so many messages all screaming 'you need to have this' if you want to be happy!

3 The Paradox of UNDERSTANDING

You can't fully understand others if you don't understand your self

In fact understanding others IS understanding our self. Often we declare our perplexity when we claim, "I just don't understand them. I thought I knew them, but now I realize I don't". What we don't realize is that the underlying cause of our inability to connect and resonate with others is our ignorance of our self. When we don't understand others we are often really saying, "I have not yet fully understood myself". We cannot read and understand the beliefs/perceptions/emotions that others are feeling until we have learned to identify the beliefs we are carrying and the true cause of the emotions that we create and feel within our self.

"When we consciously seek the deeper truths in life it's more than likely we will find paradox waiting for us at every corner."

The psychopath has no ability to empathize with others because they have spent their entire life avoiding feeling and understanding their own emotions. To know others, know self. It's not the perfect paradox in the truest sense, but it does reveal one of the truths about all our lives.

4 The Paradox of SELF INTEREST

You cannot fulfill your own interests until you serve the interests of others

All self-interest is dependent on others interests. Even if you simply want to be left alone in order to be independent, you depend on others to leave you alone! More often than not others will find ways to interfere unless you continuously reassure them and give them what they want to ensure they no longer interfere! When any country desires to act in the 'national self interest' it always depends on other countries to acquiesce and fulfill the conditions that allows the self-interested desire to be fulfilled. To act in ones' self interest requires us to first act in the interest of others.

5 The Paradox of UNIFICATION

Unity is already present...always!

We often see that within a group or community there are those who are always calling for unity. They say, "We should be united and stand as one on this". And yet they themselves are not in unity with everyone else as they themselves 'react' to the 'disunited reactions' of others. It means they are not united 'within' themselves; they are not 'at one' within themselves. They want something from the group and all 'wanting' is predicated on the false belief (albeit subconscious) that, "I am incomplete until I get what I WANT".

Paradoxically we are each already complete and we are all already united. We have simply lost our awareness of that completeness/oneness/unity. We cannot know our completeness and we cannot see or feel that unity and oneness in the world around us because we still 'believe' in division and separation. We still WANT our selves to be other than what we are. And we still WANT others and the world to be a certain way that they/it are not currently. When we are not feeling complete and when the world and others do not appear as one, it's because we create and sustain perceptions of fragmentation and division. Only when we resolve our inner, perceptual fragmentation (the voices of many self identities and the consequent desires of each identity) can we see and know the underlying completeness of our self and the underlying oneness of 'us all' everywhere... at all times! All is seldom what it appears to be and 'reality' is usually found behind the superficiality of appearances!

6 The Paradox of SELF-LIMITATION

You can never know your limitations

You can never truly know your limitations until you transcend them i.e. break through them. And if you keep breaking through your limitations there is the possibility you may realize the deeper truth, which is that you have none. Yes at a physical level there can be finite limitations of movement and skill etc. But at a mental level and spiritual level there is no limit to our capacity. To say that's as far as I will be able to grow/develop mentally or spiritually is only a 'limitation of imagination' or an imagined limitation! To say that's as far as I have ever gone and therefore will go, is 'limitation by memory' and to 'see' the future only in terms of the past. You can never fully know your limits until you transcend them and then they are no longer your limits! A classic paradox!

7 The Paradox of RAISING YOUR CONCIOUSNESS

To raise you're conscious awareness you have
to stay grounded

To raise ones consciousness means to refine or fine-tune the quality and depth of ones own self-awareness. This naturally creates a deeper awareness of what is occurring within the 'being' of the 'other'. You are also able to generate and radiate a higher quality of energy in the form of more refined thoughts and feelings. But it's not possible to raise your consciousness and fine-tune your awareness unless you remain grounded, which means you consistently and fully deal with daily events, relationships and tasks.

Many make the mistake of isolating themselves from the world and putting all their time and attention into mystical and meditative practises with the hope of simply 'rising above it all' and achieving some kind of enlightenment. They believe this is the way to be more spiritual. They believe that if they achieve this kind of enlightenment they will have transcended the mundane and set themselves free of the routine, the drudgery and the ordinary. Then they wonder why progress is fleeting and slow!

Then, one day, they realize that the real lessons that need to be learned and integrated in order to be able to 'rise above' lie in everyday places, everyday interactions with people and the everyday practicalities of living. When people, places and practicalities are not dealt with accurately, and with the energy of love, they become a burden carried within our consciousness in the form of 'unfinished business'. This burden becomes an inner weight making it impossible to raise the quality of our conscious awareness, which really means liberate our self from our attachment to the material stuff of life. Unfinished business keeps 'pulling' our thoughts and generating emotional disturbances. Sometimes this is referred to as 'your karma'.

You cannot check out of the supermarket without knowing the price of each item and paying the bill fully. Only then are the groceries completely held and carried by you, and only then can you choose and be fully in control of where and when to set them down, thus relieving yourself of part of the burden that keeps YOU on the ground! Otherwise you will be using all our energy to fearfully stay 'on the run' as you hide from the store manager or the police!

If we keep avoiding any unresolved issues in our day-to-day life we rack up mental and emotional unpaid bills in the form of our own recurring thoughts and feelings. They will only chase us for payment (resolution), thereby stopping us from raising the quality of our consciousness, which essentially means 'being internally free'.

This is why so many of us are not consistently happy on the inside. We are not free beings. We carry the karmic burden of unfinished business.

In essence, if you want to raise your consciousness and rise above the mundane and the ordinariness of the world you will need to take the world with you...for a while at least! Yet another of those pesky paradoxes!

Question:
Which of the above paradoxes did you find most
relevant to your life now?

Reflection:
To resolve a paradox you need to go beyond thinking about it in order
to 'see' it. Hence the purpose of meditation is to quieten the
thinking mind and watch what arises from the heart.

Action:
In what ways could 'the seeing' of each of the above paradoxes change the
way you 'live your life?' Make two columns, list the paradoxes
in the left hand column then list the changes they
could bring to your life in the right hand column.

Have YOU Realized the Futility of Comparison?

We live in the era of 'multilevel comparison'! At the touch of a few keys we can compare prices and services of almost anything from electricity to houses, from cars to camels, from lifestyles to lobotomies! It's a brilliant benefit of the technological age that allows us to use both time and money more efficiently. But the growing 'comparison habit' tends not to stop at commodities and utilities.

As we spectate the world through a multitude of media windows we also find ourselves easily trapped in personal comparisons with others. Either consciously or subconsciously many of us will spend huge chunks of our life in search of an identity. We will watch others, compare our self with others, desire to be like others, as we aspire to an identity that matches theirs.

As we search for our identity, sometimes we are torn between trying to be like someone else or completely rebelling against all established identity types - stereotypical or otherwise! Some will naively believe they have found their 'individuality' by being the same as someone else! They don't notice their contradiction! They believe they are a trendsetter, even while they continue to imitate others!

People Watching
Comparing our self with others is one of our most popular pastimes and disempowering habits. Usually learned at an early age, it is fed and encouraged by the marketing and entertainment

industries. Cars, bodies, homes, friends, lifestyles and characters are only a few of the many levels at which we learn to measure our self against another. In so doing it seldom feels like our self-esteem becomes stronger, and if it does, it is more than likely to be a short lived inflation of our ego, and deflation must follow.

As we watch, we compare, as we compare, we desire, and as we desire we lose our ability to be content with where we are and what we have. Someone else's life always look better than 'my life', someone else's success always seems much greater than 'my achievements'. And someone else's future always seems to look much rosier than 'my future'. These thought patterns are fatal to our wellbeing. Over time they will drain our enthusiasm, deplete our creativity and paralyze our ability to think clearly for ourselves.

Perfectly Formed Bodies

Although there are many levels at which we learn to compare, perhaps the most common is at the level of form. The 'beauty myth' feeds us the illusion that it's only when we are drop dead stunningly gorgeous that we can be successful and therefore happy. The images of perfectly formed bodies, with the most attractive faces, the perfect blemish free skin, the tingly white teeth, adorn the billboards, our glossy magazines (womens and mens) and, in some places, our daily newspaper. The underlying message is one we all now recognize and it goes like this: *If you do not look like this beautiful and happy human being then you cannot be successful and you cannot be happy.*

As we absorb this mythology many will spend both money and time attempting to achieve the shape, smile, suntan and lifestyle of the 'beautiful people'. It all comes with that subtle promise of happiness and success. If our awareness is dim enough, we will believe it, and then be perplexed as to why we become even unhappier, and even more discontent, when we obviously fail to look like the manufactured image of the perfected human being.

The sadness at not achieving what we perceive others have achieved, the disappointment at not being able to duplicate the physical beauty of another, can only result in a growing sorrow and perhaps, over time, depression. That's when the other industries step in and benefit from our failed aspirational expenditure and we attempt to counter our flagging feelings of self worth with vacations, spas, beauty parlors, gymnasiums, or a long stay at the bar! It is, for many, an unrecognized downward spiral into unhappiness.

"While it's good to see the other's virtues, and 'think' about how to develop such characteristics, it pays to leave the actual person outside the doorway of our mind."

Imitation or Inspiration

However, there are those who will counter all this and say that it's good to aspire to the heights that others seem to have reached in their life. They maintain it's good to have such 'role models' and to actually model their ways! Here is where we meet a fine line between imitation and inspiration.

To recognize the best in others, to see the virtue in another's character, is to create the kind of vision of another that can inspire us to bring the best out in our self. But while it's virtuous to see the virtues of another, and to use that awareness as inspiration for the enhancement of our own character, it pays to leave the actual person outside the doorway of our mind. Imitation may be a form of flattery but it can also be a sign that we are using the 'idea' of a 'successful them' to suppress the real potential of our self. It is a subtle form of self-sabotage. Sometimes not so subtle!

Aspirations and Inclinations

An 'aspiration' towards excellence, an inclination to inculcate virtue, an intention to replace our vicious cycles with virtuous cycles at the level of thought, feeling, attitude and action, is the road to being all that we can be. However, it is a road we must ultimately walk alone. It is not a road travelled by trying to be like someone else.

It is not a road to more acquisition or accumulation. It is a journey towards the realization that each and every one of us is already all that we can ever be, we are already complete, we are already worthy with a virtuous character that, when fully brought forth from inside out, would appear to be 'beautiful' to others. It's just that we have temporarily lost awareness of it. We have lost our capacity to live it! Even the most criminal of criminals, with a long history of violence, have within them the virtues and the values that make up the goodness of a human being. They only find it hard to believe that such goodness lives deep within. As do we, when we hear about their history! But there are many tales of redemption and the rediscovery of the beauty of the soul within the most 'unbeautiful' characters. Such tales are an inspiration.

Everyone is Unique
Ending all comparison with others is essential to living a contented and fulfilling life, where our life is 'filled full' from inside out, not outside it. To break the habit of seeking fulfillment 'out there', where it can never be found; to end the frequent moments of inevitable failure that it must bring; it helps to remember three things:

1 You are unique (it is the one thing we ALL have in common!) and it is impossible to look or be the same as anyone else.

2 Your life is a gift and an opportunity to plough your own furrow, lay down your own path, shape your own destiny, and in so doing you will do what you are here to do, which is 'create' your life, which, if you do it well, will enrich the lives of others.

3 You already have all that you need within you. Much of what your body needs comes from outside you, but ALL that YOU need comes from within, and you can never lose it, only lose your awareness of it, and access to it!

It also helps to keep reminding your self that what you see in the bathroom mirror in the morning is not you (at last, good news!) it is just the form you 'occupy'. It means beauty is not skin deep. It is beyond the skin, prior to the skin. It means beauty is not an image or a reflection, it is what you see and feel when you realize and know yourself as a source of love and a maker of peace. It is what you are when you use your spiritual energy, which is you, to guide others to the same awareness.

Your beauty is what others will see and feel when your thoughts and actions are shaped by love, guided by truth and shared with kindness. Then virtue will be its own reward from inside out, as well as bringing it's own rewards, from outside in! Then all comparisons with others and all aspiration to be like others will not only cease, they will be recognized for what they are, a fearful attempt to stay at the shallow end of the pool wondering what it might be like to swim freely in it's depths.

To be your self, get deep, and never compare your self with others!

Question:
In what areas or at what levels do you find yourself
comparing yourself with others most.

Reflection:
When it comes to creating your life what is the difference between aspiration,
inspiration and perspiration.

Action:
See the beauty (the virtue) within the actions of one person every day
this week , and where appropriate, tell them what you saw.

Why Are YOU Late...Again?

Do you have a compulsive latecomer in your life? It doesn't matter how much notice you give them they still arrive late. Even if you attempt to trick them into believing the meeting is earlier than officially scheduled, they will still confound you as they contrive to wander in well after it's begun. And even if you attempt to accompany them personally to the meeting, just to ensure they walk through the door on time, there comes a moment when you realize they have slipped over the horizon and out of sight, as they conveniently remember something life threatening has been forgotten, or a minor emergency has been telepathically received!

Office Introvert

Offices and teams, families and friends, often have a compulsive latecomer. They always seem to arrive just at the moment when key points will have to be repeated to bring them exclusively up to speed. Usually they stroll in with a slight 'fluster' that implies they have just dragged themselves away from having saved some part of the world... again! They may even carry that self important look combined with the slightly disdainful facial expression and body language that says, "God how boring and uninteresting lives you all must lead to actually be punctual and on time... all the time!"

Even if the compulsive latecomer is also the office introvert, and they are as shy and retiring as a vampire at sunrise, they may be someone who quietly soaks up the rippling waves of animosity that are often hiding behind apparent warm and welcoming smiles. They will probably even covet the attention and energy from the team's most skillful sarcastic commentator when they say, "So glad you could make it", in a manner that is obviously as far from gladness as the Earth is from Jupiter's fifth moon!

While it's easy to become frustrated by the compulsive latecomer, there are usually underlying reasons for this particular behavior, which they may not be aware of themselves. If we can recognize the reason it may provide us with a deeper 'understanding' of their habit, which then allows us to remain a little more detached and unflustered. We can then create a strategy to respond more effectively to the latecomer's addiction.

Here are seven reasons why some people habitually turn up well after proceedings have begun.

1 No Sense of Clock Time

Somewhere in their dim and distant past they learned that clock time is just not that important. It's only a clock after all! Perhaps a parent passed on a sense of 'supper can always wait' as they demonstrated that building a go-cart in the garden shed was much more important than a prescheduled event like dinner. They learned to allow themselves to be so absorbed in a task that they easily lose all sense of clock time. Sometimes we call this the early stirrings of creative genius!

2 Attempting Control

The latecomer soon learns they will 'get a reaction' when they are late. They begin to develop the false belief, albeit subconsciously, that they are able to control others behaviors, even if invisible daggers are flying their way. Coming late, and thereby triggering an emotional reaction, gives them a false sense of power.

3 Attention Seeking

To some people any attention is good attention, even if it's hatred. Some time in their past, usually when knee high to the proverbial grasshopper, the only way to get attention was by acting against the will or approval of others. Coming late is one such behavior when they know they will become the center of attention, albeit grumpy attention, for a few moments at least. Thus their existence is affirmed.

> *"Regular lateness gives them a history, a personal reputation, from which a sense of identity can be shaped."*

4 Self Importance

When people obviously glare and complain at the latecomers arrival it gives the latecomer a sense of identity, "I am famous for being the latecomer around here". This label and ongoing story of their regular lateness gives them a history, a personal reputation, from which a sense of identity can be shaped. They use their label and story to build and sustain a perverted sense of self-importance. But it's all in their mind. These are the subtle games of the ego of which they are unlikely to be even dimly aware.

5 Personal Inadequacy

Perhaps coming late is a confidence issue. Coming on time would mean their self-image was positive, their actions accurate and they were respectful towards others. But if their self-image is one of being inadequate with low self-esteem and self-respect, then such behaviors as always arriving late will emerge as an expression of that negative self-image. The self-image of inadequacy and failure, which has become 'comfortable' over time, must be sustained. Coming on time would mean their self-image is changing. That would be uncomfortable! Unknowingly they remain in their comfort zone, which is already uncomfortable! Better the discomfort you know than a discomfort you don't know!

6 Plain Lazy

Or perhaps it's just good old fashioned laziness! They have a 'can't be bothered' attitude to most things, especially anything to do with work. Somewhere in the past, being bothered and making the effort was either ridiculed or frowned upon. Or work itself is seen as a necessary evil that just has to be survived and no more. Laziness has a number of deep reasons and its zestless attitude can spread like a virulent strain of flu. Laziness is a sure sign motivation has been and continues to be deeply suppressed.

7 Timeless Consciousness

Sometimes you encounter someone who is truly in a timeless state of consciousness. It seems to be the hardest thing for them to be time conscious. It's as if no one ever taught them how to read and use a clock. For them the future is never a worry or even a concern. It will come when it comes and whatever it brings is just fine. So wandering into the meeting, or arriving for 'the date', whenever they feel like it, is so natural for them. They have no ulterior motive. They have no worry or fear of what others will think. And they have no intention to do it in order to get attention. They are truly free spirits for whom we can all learn how to not take life and those 'darn clocks' so seriously.

Understanding why the latecomer is compulsively late allows us to shift from condemnation to compassion, and therefore not to lose the plot the next time they wander in well after they could have. Otherwise we can easily become the 'serial complainer' ourself. Then, even when they are early, we may even turn that into, "Look at you, always early or on time. Can't you relax and let go a bit more?"

When there are deeper subconscious reasons for why the latecomer is compulsively late, it's as if they know not what they do. Even if it appears that they think they do know what they do, they usually don't!

Then of course there is that rare, enlightened soul for whom time is just a mental construct to which most people learn to become attached and dependent. But not them! For them there is no such thing as 'late', or early, for that matter. They have realized and seen through the three illusions that run the world.

- Hurry up, time is running out!
- If we do it quickly we can 'save time'!
- Leave it till later; there should be 'more time' tomorrow!

Maybe that's why we seldom meet such a soul in many meetings at all! What's the point in hanging around with people who have not yet realized and seen through the illusion that we sometimes call the 'importance of time'? After all, how can a mental construct that generates anxiety ever be important!

Question:
Which of the above reasons do you think applies to the person in your life that appears to be suffering from 'perpetual latecomers syndrome'?

Reflection:
In the larger 'scheme of things' why might there be no such thing as 'arriving late'.

Action:
Create a proactive behavioral strategy towards your compulsive latecomer that will convey a positive response and not a negative reaction i.e. whereby you are not emotionally affected by their apparent lateness.

Vision, Goal, Dream or Desire
What's the Difference?

Apparently, some years ago at Yale University, final year students were asked a range of questions about their life. Within the study were two significant questions. The first was, "Do you have goals?" Around ten per cent said yes they did. The second question was, "If you have goals, do you have them written down and do something about them every day?" Around four per cent of the total said yes to this. Twenty years later the University decided to find out where all those questioned were in their lives.

The search spanned the world, and while some had died the vast majority were found and completed the follow-up questionnaire. It turned out that the four per cent who had written their goals 20 years before were streets ahead of the rest when the indicators of success were examined. They had achieved a more balanced life, their wellbeing and commitment to the community were, apparently, 'outstandingly different' from the rest. And while financial worth is by no means a true measure of success, the 4 per cent were worth more than the other 96 per cent together!

Perhaps the most interesting interpretation of this study is that when it is globally translated it appears that around 96 per cent of us will spend our lives helping the other 4 per cent achieve their goals!

Variety of Visions

While a goal is a kind of vision (mental picture of a future achievement) a vision is seldom a goal. While a goal tends to be a fixed aim towards which certain actions are carried out, vision takes many forms. It takes *historical vision* to know where you have been, *situational vision* to see where you are and *strategic vision* to work out the direction in which you should now be going. Vision, in this sense, is a kind of multidimensional contextual awareness that may or may not provide clarity.

"The vision of tomorrow tends to be open and malleable, able to alter it's depth and texture as new information arrives from outside in and as insight arises from inside out!"

A *strategic vision* can be either based on an awareness of current patterns and trends and how they may be integrated to form the future, or it can simply be an intuitive awareness of what is going to occur and the process by which it will happen.

From Narrow to Broad

In the context of the future, a goal is fixed and vision is malleable. A goal tends to be a target that is grounded and focused at one point in 'the tomorrow' of time and space. If it changes it then ceases to be 'that goal', but a new goal is created. Whereas the vision of tomorrow tends to be open and malleable, able to alter it's depth and texture, as new information arrives from outside in and as insight arises from inside out!

While a goal tends to be narrow and highly defined, a vision tends to be broad with some elements that may remain vague and ambiguous. A variety of factors may enhance, enrich and deepen the vision of the 'way things will be' between 'here' and its manifestation or realization.

Often, both a goal and a vision tend to be confused with 'desire'. We say 'goal' or 'vision' when we really mean 'desire'. When desire arises it means that fear enters the arena – the fear that I may fail to achieve my goal or manifest the vision. It is the thought, "I might not get/achieve what I want", that weakens the power and the magnetism of the goal/vision. That is not to say desire will not get you to your goal. It can, and many will testify to 'desire power' as they pass on their advice in the form of, "You have to truly want it".

However, others remind us that when 'I want' the achievement of the goal it also means we are probably making our happiness dependent on reaching the goal, which means our happiness is perpetually delayed. It is always 'then' and seldom now! The journey between here and there is usually a process of anxiety in some form or other.

Happiness is not the Goal!

This anxiety then sabotages the quality of energy required to reach the goal effectively, which may explain why those that do 'want it bad enough' are not so happy, and usually a bit stressed, 'on the way there'! They are more likely to struggle and strive their way there. When they do arrive and allow themselves a few moments of contented happiness, it's not long before they are driving themselves on again to the next goal (desired outcome/achievement) so that they may have the justification to be happy again! Sometimes this is known as the 'protestant work ethic'! Which implies you have to work extremely hard and 'achieve' before you can 'deserve' to be happy.

By contrast, that other frequently quoted saying reminds us to march to the drum of a deeper truth, "Happiness is not the goal, happiness is the way to the goal".

Conceive and Believe

A dream is also a vision but tends to contain such high aspirations and desires that place it beyond what is realistic and into the bounds of the impossible. When some do achieve their dream and say "I am living my dream". It usually means they are fulfilling their greatest desire. In fact they dared to dream, they dared to create such a vision for their life that while it may have sounded 'too much to expect' to the ears of others,

> *"The emergence of a clear vision can take days, weeks or months or it can happen in seconds."*

they wanted it so badly and believed in it so deeply, it became a reality. They remind us all that if you believe in what you conceive you will achieve. While we all have the ability to conceive 'our dream', it's our lack of belief, the weakness of our conviction, which can let us down.

The dream becomes either a fantasy into which we escape or simply wishful thinking.

A true vision on the other hand emerges into consciousness with a sense of clarity and certainty. The visionary 'knows' this is what will be; this is what will come about. There is no personal burning desire to 'make it happen' but a deep knowing it 'will happen'. There is an internal confidence that if one 'holds' the vision and allows it to inform decisions and actions, it will come to be, easily and naturally.

The visionary is aware the vision is a picture of that which will manifest 'out there' in the future of time and space, but it is a reality now 'in here' within their consciousness. The power of that 'present reality', if it is free of mental and emotional interference, is then 'stepped down' and translated into actions that will contribute to the crystallization of the vision in the visible world.

Rational and Intuitive Cues!

A powerful personal vision is usually a composite of elements and is more caught than taught. Vision formation is internal, and it requires a sifting, a recognition, an ability to give priority while synthesizing many elements - some of which may be barely visible to the inner eye. It is a process of focusing or patterning, drawing from a variety of kaleidoscopic sources including the influences of others, of personal experiences and reflections. Clarity of vision is enhanced by 'pattern recognition and selection', which is a process that requires both rational and intuitive cues. The emergence of a clear vision can take days, weeks or months or it can happen in seconds.

All of which require what is often called the 'eye of the intellect'. It is the intellect that sees and discerns the patterns, next to the reflections, alongside the intuitions, while holding a backdrop of experiences and insperiences, as it both creates as well as allows the vision to crystalize in consciousness. The clarity of such an intellect depends on freedom from uncontrolled thoughts (usually desires) and emotional disturbance. Hence the ancient practise of meditation, long recognized as the most effective way to open the 'third eye' (intellect) and sharpen the intellects discernment.

Catalyzing Unity

In a turbulent world, a clear and powerful vision can induce stability and restore a semblance of order and direction. That's why 'vision' is probably the most common attribute amongst leaders who have been able to communicate that vision in a way that inspires others, while showing them the future and catalyzing unity on the way!

However, those with powerful and inspirational visions probably need to be careful regarding when, where and with whom to share. History shows us that if the vision is in opposition to the 'status quo' it can trigger resistance in those who are threatened by vision-driven change. Their resistance can be fatal. JFK, King and Gandhi are the most public examples on the international stage whose clarity and consistency of vision attracted violent resistance.

But daily 'vision resistance' can be found more commonly across breakfast and boardroom tables. Which is why it is often best to create it, sustain it and keep quiet about it. And just enjoy watching it become a reality.

In the meantime, it's never a bad idea to follow the often-quoted advice of Goethe, another wise old soul when he said:

"Concerning all acts of initiative (and creation) there is one elementary truth, the ignorance of which kills countless ideas and splendid plans – that's the moment one definitely commits oneself, and then providence moves too. All sorts of things occur to help one that would not otherwise have occurred. A whole stream of events issues forth from the decision, raising in one's favor all manner of unforeseen incidents and meetings and material assistance which no man could have dreamt would come his way. Whatever you can do, or dream, begin it! Boldness has genius, magic and power in it. Begin It Now.

Question:
What do you feel is most powerfully emerging in your
consciousness – a vision, a dream or a goal?

Reflection:
Take a moment to write it down, reflect on it,
and refine it on paper.

Action:
As you hold your vision/dream/goal in your mind,
what action is it calling you to do now?

Are YOU Making the Shift from FORCE to POWER?

"You have to make things happen if you want to see results... you have to reach for the stars... just go out and get it while you can... ask your self how much do you really want it...don't let anything or anyone stand in your way!" These are all motivational clichés to which many refer as they 'force' their way through life and encourage others to do the same. And they do work to motivate some of us. The highly ambitious worker can climb all the way to the top executive seat; the aspiring and talented sports person can become a world champion; the driven businessman or woman can build a commercial empire; the naive teenage political activist can become a prime minister.

But at what cost? Some would say no cost at all, if it's what you really want. Go live your dream they say! They consider all the effort as an investment. For others it's at great cost as it may require the sacrifice of a relationship, or perhaps doing what, deep down, they don't really want to do, or behaving in ways that contradict their innate values. All to get to where they 'believe' they should be. It's a belief that is often blindly assimilated from the prevailing culture in which they find themselves.

So much depends on how you define success. Some definitions of success have a built in guarantee of a stressful journey. It's been claimed that if you really aspire to be not just good at something, but achieve excellence, you will need to spend 10,000 hours in focused practise, or thereabouts. But what lies behind practise? Some are driven by the desire to prove to themselves they can do it. This is force. Others push themselves with a neediness to be recognized. This is also force. Others practise out of the pure joy of the practising itself. This is power. One is draining and the other is energizing. Both may achieve excellence, but one is likely to arrive used up and worn out, while the other arrives with a skip in their step and a twinkle in their eye! Their joy is undiminished.

"Stress is usually the companion of force. Force doesn't typify the truly loving partner or spouse, the intelligent manager or the caring parent."

Are You a Human Doing?

The way of force is generally the route we are taught to take to achieve success in life. Whether it's a work ethic that is built into the prevailing culture or just an overly ambitious parent. Force is the most celebrated way to fulfill your ambition and your destiny. However, as a way of living it usually turns out not to be the most enlightened and, therefore, not the happiest. As a way of 'relating' it's not the most effective, as it will likely involve some manipulation and end in distrust. As a way of 'acting' it's not the most energizing. As a way of 'achieving' it's more the way of a 'human doing' as a result of forgetting we are first and foremost a 'human being.' The action addicts and the rushaholics are the flag carriers for the forceful way to do life.

We know we are forcing things when we notice and feel that events and relationships are not flowing smoothly. That's why force is seldom the sign of a happy and contented individual. Their life is usually a testimony to constant striving, frequently struggling and often a lot of shoving others aside! It doesn't signal someone who is living in a relaxed and natural way. Nor someone who considers others in kind or compassionate ways!

Force doesn't typify the truly loving partner or spouse, the intelligent manager or the caring parent. When operating from force they all become quite grumpy as soon as they don't get their way. Stress and frequent grumpiness are usually primary symptoms of the strategy of force!

So what then is the alternative to forcing your way through life? What other ways are there, to live without needing to be someone who is regularly pushing, insisting, manipulating, striving, struggling, cajoling and perhaps emotionally blackmailing others?

There are shifts that you can make into easiness and flow, into a gentler and more effective way to use your energy and cruise through your life. They are the shifts from 'force to power.' They are shifts that often involve a change of belief or belief system, so that a new mindset may take form. This then alters the way you perceive, think and act.

Here are some of those shifts, which also give you the chance to review your own mindsets and spot if you are currently living from force or from your power.

1 The Shift from OBJECTS to PEOPLE

Force is to see and treat people as if they are objects, a type of resource, just to get a job done. Whereas power is to see and respond to people as human beings! It starts with your vision of the other! How do you consider the other, perceive the other, create the other, within your consciousness. If you see them as someone to do something for you, achieve something for you, then you will likely see them as an object, even though you 'appear' to appreciate them for who they are. From that vision expectations and desires arise. That's when we start to overtly try to push and manipulate someone into doing what we want, or believe should be done.

Both our attitude and behavior will start to become forceful. They will sense you are not connecting with them as a person but as a resource that serves your needs. This is at the heart of many workplace cultures. Hence the term Human Resources! Which is one reason why the workplace is often not such a happy place, but a space of fractured and conflicted relationships.

Power, on the other hand, is to hold a vision of the other as a person, as a human being, acknowledging their feelings and aspirations, needs and desires. From this arises care, an authentic appreciation of the other, empathy towards the other, respect for the other, which translates into time and attention given to the other. It's the power of these attitudes that serves the other, empowers both the self and the other, and builds a stable relationship.

2 The Shift from CONTROL to INFLUENCE

Force is to attempt to control what you cannot control (usually other people) whereas power is developing and applying of the skills of influence.

Many of us seem to grow up learning one fatal lesson, that other people are responsible for our happiness. This misbelief shapes our primary intention within many of our relationships, which is to ensure others do or say or be or give us what we want, so that we can be happy. Which really means free us from our unhappiness! And so we start to try to control others, which means force others. It starts in our minds with our mental vocabulary, which sounds like 'they should' or 'they must' or 'they have to.' And it ends in our emotional disappointment when they don't!

Yet sometimes they do 'seem' to do or be or give you what you want. That's when you mistakenly believe you 'made them.' That's also when you create the illusion (belief) that you are controlling them. This makes you lazy within the relationship. Then there arrives that moment when they stop dancing to your tune and you become frustrated, resentful and disillusioned. We become lazy, which then sabotages our ability to learn how to connect authentically and be a beneficial influence for others. Many parents and managers, whose job it is to 'influence', fall into this 'laziness trap.' They 'believe' they are in control, but they're not!

"Force is to believe that resistance is the way to change what does not appear to be right. Whereas acceptance is a powerful first step to influencing the direction of change by accepting what is!"

We all seem prone to attempt to force others at some point in our relationships. We fail to cultivate the attitudes and skills that are most influential. But how do you do that? Well, the first step is to stop trying to control others and the world. Not a small step for many. When you do give up trying to control what cannot be controlled (other people and any events more than three feet away!) you will notice the disappearance of most of your stress! The second step is learning and practicing the actual skills of influence. But that's another workshop! It's called life!

3 The Shift from RESISTANCE to ACCEPTANCE

Acceptance is the primary influencing skill and essential to any relationship that requires repair. Force is to believe that resistance is the way to change what does not appear to be right. Whereas acceptance is a powerful first step to influencing the direction of change by accepting what is! While resistance tends to focus on the past, acceptance focuses on the present and the future. The precursor to all resistance is the emotion of fear, and all fear comes from the ego. So all resistance is essentially a progeny of the ego.

It seems many of us will live our entire life in a state of resistance simply because we all learn to create an ego. Ego is just a false sense of self. It's a misidentification. It's created the moment we lose our sense of self in an idea or image in our own minds. We try to build an identity out of what we are not! We don't realize that everything that we are not changes! Everything that we are not will either be lost, damaged, threatened or moved. So when we identify with what we are not we learn to believe that we i.e. our self, can be and will be damaged, threatened, moved or lost!

As a consequence, we distort the energy of our consciousness into fear. We create and feel the emotion of fear. And it's always fear that generates resistance in our relationship with just about everything and everyone.

Some develop this fear so profoundly they go deeply inside themselves and close up completely. They resist all attempts to open them. Most of us muddle through, tolerating our anxieties without realizing we do so! We relieve the unhappiness that must come with our fear induced resistances by indulging in various drugs like entertainment, food, shopping, and perhaps other people! We all have our reliefs and escapes!

All conflict is born of the mutual resistance between two people, or two groups of people, which then escalates. Life only really begins when we realize acceptance is the only way to relate to everyone and everything while maintaining some form of happiness. Acceptance does not mean you agree with the other or condone what the other may have done. To accept 'the all' as it is, and 'them all' as they are, is to allow your self to create the deepest happiness from inside out, otherwise known as contentment! Fear, in all it's forms, gradually disappears along the way.

4 The Shift from TELLING to ASKING

This happens when you realize that while it 'seems' you can have 'power over' others, **in reality**, you don't and you can't. But you can have 'power with'! Force is telling, telling, telling, and no one loves a dictator, whereas power is the art of 'intelligent asking' so that others discover their own internal resources and create their own way. This is the heart of the art of coaching, and the building of relationships based on trust, respect and understanding.

It's fairly obvious that when you move into telling mode you are trying to force what you believe and think onto and into the other! Well, perhaps not when you've been asked to share some information, or you are passing on the latest news or perhaps something about what you are feeling. 'Telling' is force when it is imposing or ordering or demanding or expecting. But these ways of communication

"TELLING is force when it is imposing or ordering or demanding or expecting, but these can be cleverly disguised ways of communication with the intention to manipulate the other."

can often be cleverly disguised. They can be delivered softly and seductively. But when they come with the intention to manipulate the other it means we have reverted to 'trying to control' mode.

While the listener may start in an open and receptive state, if you don't soften your 'telling' it won't be long before ears close and minds switch off. Ask any parent of teenagers! One of the great secrets of ensuring a relationship will flourish is ask, ask, ask. It's an invitation to open up. It is to say 'I value your thoughts' which is code for 'I value you'. It is to demonstrate 'I am open to you', it is to extend respect to the other. It is to empower them as they share what's on their mind. We all seem to intuitively know this is the most powerful way to connect and cultivate any and all relationships. But we forget! What makes us forget is usually our judgment of the other! Notice whenever you judge another not only do you lose your inner peace you also lose your respect for the other. You are back in 'force' mode!

Making the transition from force to power requires an ongoing enhancement of self-awareness. Only then can we start to recognize the moments and the behaviors we are creating that represent a forceful approach. The main symptoms to be aware of are any emotional reactions, any resistant behaviors, any feelings of unhappiness and any thoughts that sound like, "I am not getting what I want."

From force to power is not a technique. It's an awakening awareness that is a natural precursor to new behaviors and deeper, more enlightened ways of relating.

Push the pause button and raise your awareness for a few moments by considering the following:

Question:
Assuming we can all make all four of the above shifts,
which one do you sense you need to make the most?

Reflection:
What are your two most frequent behaviors that tell
you that you are attempting to force things?

Action:
Pick three people you frequently see, recall the ways in which you behave
towards them that are forceful, visualize what would be non-forceful
and then practise in those relationships this coming week.

The Invasion of Force

We live in a world where force is cultivated and celebrated in almost all areas of society - the force of the warmongers, of political movements, of religious zealotry, of economic manipulation, of environmental exploitation, of media hype, of sporting success. Our worship of speed almost guarantees an extremely unrelaxed life as we try to force our way into the future faster today than we did yesterday! That, in turn, requires we force more energy out of the natural world to sustain our addictions to speed and superficiality at the cost of substance and value.

The invasive force of entertainment, and the advertising that comes with it, is essentially about people using emotional manipulation to try to force us to create more emotions of our own to which we ourselves become addicted. Most fictional narratives, projected by the dramas of movies and television, are about people trying to force others to do what they want! As a consequence we learn that life is, by definition, an exercise in forcefulness. We tend to learn that success has to be, can only be, the result of force!

> *"Most fictional narratives, projected by the dramas of movies and television, are about people trying to force others to do what they want!"*

The force of marketing has, as it's mission, to make us believe that we want what we don't need! Their business is to continuously try to force our perceptions and aspirations into a place where they can manipulate our decisions.

Power Restored

Power, on the other hand, is exercised when we decide not to succumb mentally and emotionally to such forces. Power is our own capacity to discern and to 'see through' the attempted manipulations of others. Power is exercised when we are able to remain calm and uninfluenced by the emotional exhortations projected at us through the many windows of a media driven world. Power is exercised when success is realized to be the mastery of our state of being, and not just another achievement in the world.

We obviously can't control those many external forces that attempt to invade and shape our lives. We can only make choices about how we will live our own life day-by-day, moment-by-moment, in relation to such forces. But we do have choices at almost every moment.

Here are the five further crucial shifts from 'force to power' in the ways that we use our energies in our own personal life.

5 The Shift from TAKING to GIVING

We are all on the take! Well, maybe not all of us, not all of the time, not in all situations. But 'taking' is the inherited programming most of us seem to have assimilated. Believing life is 'for the taking' and things have to be grabbed while you can, underpins many of our forceful ways of living. Opportunities should be 'taken' when they come, another person should be 'taken' into your life,

Power is our own capacity to discern and to 'see through' the attempted manipulations of others.

money should be 'taken' to live life, things should be 'taken' to create a comfortable life, get as much as you can if you want to be successful, are all mindsets that guarantee we will try to force life itself to deliver unto us exactly what we want, often justified as what we need!

Some enlightened souls have realized that always thinking about what 'I want' and always trying to get, acquire, possess and accumulate for 'me', is only going to lead to the 'misery emotions' such as anxiety, tension, disappointment and anger. Not to mention the pressure to maintain the flow of our accumulations. Such souls have glimpsed a deeper truth, which reminds us we are not here to take but to give of our self, extend our being, share our energies. It's nature's way.

They would remind us that 'to give' is human natures primary impulse. They have realized the 'power of giving' and that paradoxically it's only in true giving that real love is generated and known. It's in that loving state, they say, that we also find our sense of authentic security that many of us mistakenly seek from 'things' and people in the world. They claim that the love of giving and giving with love is what empowers ones self from inside out. Many would probably agree, if only intuitively at first!

6 The Shift from CONDEMNATION to COMPASSION

We don't tend to notice how unrelaxed we become whenever we judge and condemn another person or some far-flung event. Even if it's just something or someone we see on TV. It's not easy to see why and how judgment can be such a forceful state. We can be so quick to condemn the crimes of others, the emotions of others, the decisions of others, the smallest actions of others.

Our judgment and subsequent condemnation blind us to the reality that others make mistakes, usually due to unwise decisions, simply because they have temporarily lost access to their own innate wisdom. They have assimilated a programmed set of beliefs in their head, usually from their childhood yesterday, that is shaping their actions today. But we don't 'see' that, we can't see that, as we projectively force our judgments at them.

Whenever we condemn not only do we make our self peaceless, and somewhat upset, we suffer from an unhappiness based on our doomed attempt to force others to see it, do it, be it, according to 'my way'! It doesn't matter how right we may believe we are, it is still a form of arrogance. And it's all happening in our own heads.

Compassion has no chance of entering our consciousness, at least until the emotions behind our judgmental condemnation are dissolved. The power of compassion arises from acceptance and understanding. It arises when we stop trying to judge and fix others and the world in our own minds and realize that 'the all' and 'the everything' out there, while far from perfection, is unfolding as it does, as it will, as it 'should'. And that any form of violence by others is not a reason to condemn, but an opportunity to understand that it's just a sign that they are asleep, unaware and unenlightened, and in a state of internal suffering within themselves.

"BELIEFS are what we 'think' is true (but don't 'know' is true) whereas values are what we 'care about' at any given moment."

It's not so easy to see, in the moments when we set our self up as judge and jury, that our condemnation is itself a form of violence.

7 The Shift from POSITIONAL POWER to RELATIONAL POWER

Position actually means 'power' to many. Some realize that as soon as they use their position to get something done, or attempt to manipulate another, they are using force and are therefore diminishing their power! We all know those moments when we are on the end of someone using 'positional power'. They are attempting to force us to do or be something that they want for themselves. They will usually threaten us with consequences. We soon switch off within the relationship and may eventually move away from them.

'Relational power', on the other hand, is built on an acceptance of the other. It becomes the ground for cultivating mutual trust and respect. These are the strands between people through which there is an exchange, a reciprocal flow, of energy that is empowering for both parties. They form a relational foundation that doesn't shake whenever adversity calls.

Positional power is based on a form of attempted control 'over' the other. Relational power is power 'with' the other. It provides the basis for a stable and mutually respectful relationship that is capable of co-operating, co-creating and co-sustaining all that may be generated and shared by both parties.

8 The Shift from BELIEFS to VALUES

Force is to live by a set of learned beliefs and to attempt to impose those beliefs on others. Whereas power is to consciously realize your values and allow your values to guide your decisions and actions, without imposing them on others. For example, do you 'believe' in competition and therefore sustain a competitive culture? If you do you are using a forcefulness that is driven by the draining energy of fear – the fear of losing.

Or do you 'value' co-operation and therefore inspire unity of focus and action. If so, then you are using the empowering energies of love. Where there is co-operation there is unity and where there is unity there is love! Not Hollywood love, but the natural energy of the human heart that connects with others effortlessly. But as long as we 'believe' in competition this 'belief' will always sabotage our ability to generate a culture of co-operation.

The Fuel of Belief

Most of us learn to run our lives on the fuel of beliefs and belief systems. We seldom realize beliefs are static entities within our consciousness that require forcing outwards and reaffirming through our attitudes and actions. Beliefs tend to make our perceptions and behaviors rigid. Beliefs can be challenged and therefore threatened so they often require the force of defensiveness. Beliefs become our subtle attachments and they suppress our ability to spark, energize and live our values. Beliefs are what we 'think' is true (but don't 'know' is true) whereas values are what we 'care about' at any given moment. In such caring moments we are 'being true'.

When we attach our self to our beliefs, and the principles that we like to build out of our beliefs, we diminish our capacity to give, to care, for the other. The 'belief' in caring is not the same as the actual caring that arises when we truly 'value' the other. When caring is driven by the belief that's it's the right thing to do, it's more like a duty, it's a form of force. Whereas power is the care that emerges from the natural intention to look after another for no reason other than you value them.

But if we care less just because we know the other holds a different set of beliefs, that's the moment when the force of our attachment to our beliefs overcomes the power of *"Our belief in survival as the purpose of life tends to ensure we isolate our self, if not within community, then in our own consciousness."*

our capacity to value i.e. to care. This is the essence of the tension between religions. They appear to espouse the same values, which are powerful when they come through into action. But they sabotage all that by fighting over their differences in their beliefs.

Belief underlies force, whereas 'valuing' underpins power. Not power over, or more powerful than, but the power of our consciousness when we access our innate wisdom to accept, embrace and care for all others, as they are, regardless of their beliefs.

9 The Shift from SURVIVAL to SERVICE

Are you here for your self or are you here to serve others? Force will arise from the belief that life's purpose is survival. It makes us turn life into a struggle and develop the spiritual weakness known as the emotion of fear. Whereas, when life's purpose is one of 'service' then the intention and action of giving becomes the basis of our growth. It invokes, from inside out, the spiritual strength we refer to as love. When that internal strength is real then survival ceases to be an issue.

Why am I here? Why are we all here? These are questions that may flit across most minds at some stage in life. A few will seriously try to work out the meaning of life. Many of us are taught to believe that life is basically a Darwinian struggle for the survival of the fittest. We are indoctrinated in the 'me first' philosophy, the 'you better look after number one' imperative, because 'it's a crazy and dangerous world out there'!

So our default purpose becomes survival, as that's how we are taught to interpret our stay within the macrocosm of all life on planet earth. So it seems to make sense to apply it to the microcosm of our own life. What we don't notice is that survival mode equals fear mode, which equals unhappiness mode, which means the meaning of life seems to be a process of tolerating continuous unhappiness. But it's not easy to see and join those dots.

"We are indoctrinated in the 'me first' philosophy, in the 'you better look after number one' imperative, because it's a crazy and dangerous world out there."

Others however, seem to realize that we are here to serve, to give, to help, to guide... others! As this realization dawns, survival becomes a non-issue. To be of service is to make your self of value to others! That's when you know your own value. Life automatically becomes more meaningful. That's why some people give up a materially comfortable lifestyle and head off to help those with lesser comfort. They recognize the power that re-emerges from within when they make the shift from survival into service.

Once again, push the pause button and increase your own awareness by considering the following:

Question:
Assuming we can all make all five of the above shifts
which one do you sense you need to make the most?

Reflection:
Create a way to check the day gone by for moments of force
and moments of power as you reflect on
the day at the end of the day!

Action:
Find two other people, friends are recommended, take them for a cappuccino
conversation, and generate a deep discussion
around the difference between force and power.
Enlighten each other!

Are YOU Easily Impressed?

Whenever we travel we return with an overall 'impression' of our experience of our journey and destination. Sometimes the impression is not so good, while at other times we may even say, "I was so impressed with what I saw". We do the same with people. Some seem to impress us while others have the opposite effect, and we may even say, "I was not impressed with them at all".

There seems to be a spectrum of 'being impressed'. At one end there are those who are easily impressed, which really means easy to influence. It doesn't take much to win their admiration, which may eventually border on worship. While, at the other end there are those who are almost impossible to impress. They seem unmoved, regardless of the spectacle or the extent of the achievements of others or even the charisma of another. They either have a habitually negative vision of most people and events, or they have realized 'the trap' that being impressed can be.

Trapped in the Surface

How about you? Are you easy to impress? Are you frequently heard to say" "WOW... isn't that/aren't they.... just amaaaazing?" Do you fawn at the feet of someone you regard as 'special', metaphorically speaking? Or are you hard to move, hard to impress?

If you are someone who is easy to impress it probably means you have 'devotional tendencies'. Being easily impressed is not a bad thing in itself, but it can be a handicap if you are seeking to discern the deeper, more profound truths about life, the universe and, well, everything! Why, because being easily impressed means there is the tendency to get trapped on the surface of life, caught in external appearances or in the superficial features of the world or in the behaviors of others. And that blocks your ability to discern 'depth' and find deeper meaning within your self.

To understand exactly why 'being impressed' is not such good idea it's necessary to see and understand the dynamic i.e. the mechanism that takes place within our consciousness when 'impression' happens.

Shaping Up

Whenever you allow your self to become impressed, in that moment, whatever it is that you're impressed with is shaping your consciousness, which is you! When we were children we pressed shapes into plasticine and the result was the piece of plasticine was left with an impression shaping it. The original shape of the plasticine is lost. And the same happens to us when we allow ourselves, our consciousness, to be impressed. We lose the shape of our consciousness, which means we lose the mastery of our consciousness.

We lose the ability to create our own thoughts and feelings as they become shaped almost entirely by the impression we 'allowed' the person/place/event to leave. The extreme form of this is 'worship', an absolute devotion to an object, person or even to an idea, to such an extent that it both shapes the thoughts arising in our mind and it 'skews' our intellects capacity to discern and decide accurately. As a result we will start to generate 'bias' and perhaps eventually some form of 'prejudice'.

Mental Law

We could say that this is perfectly natural because this is what human beings appear to have been doing for centuries, if not thousands of years. Archeologists spend their lives picking over the artifacts of ancient peoples in an attempt to understand why they were so highly impressed, and therefore totally influenced, by someone or something. Historians spend their lives analyzing the words and actions of those individuals who refused to be impressed, and therefore influenced, by someone in particular, and everything in general.

Walk into most children's bedrooms and you are likely to find photos of their heroes, often sports, music or media personalities, are pinned to the walls. Playgrounds are displays of imitation as they dress, talk and act like the person that has impressed them most. All harmless fun we may think. Just a part of growing up we may say. But there is a mental law that says that you will become 'like' the object to which you surrender your conscious mind. In this way we can easily NOT learn how to be the master of our own consciousness, we can easily NOT learn how to be the authority of our own thoughts and feelings, we can easily NOT learn how to be our natural and free self.

"We can easily NOT learn how to be our natural and free self."

That said, the only way we can get a 'feeling' for the rightness or wrongness, appropriateness or inappropriateness, of becoming impressed, is through the lens of our own personal experience. In the spirit of self-reflection, which all these short essays seek to encourage, here are some common areas where we all tend to become impressed, and very often extremely impressed, and the effect it has. See if any ring true in your experience.

Being impressed by another's wealth serves to block the emergence of your own wealth.

Real wealth is not material. True wealth comprises your innate abilities and the qualities of your being. When those abilities/qualities, those attributes of consciousness, of self, are used in the right way at the right time they will naturally attract material wealth in return. When you become impressed by someone else's material wealth it's as if you are suppressing your self-worth and self-esteem thereby diminishing your self-respect, all of which are required to empower your own innate qualities/abilities.

Being impressed by the 'position' of another blocks your ability to relate and interact with that 'person'.

Many of us learn to respect the authority of position more than the person who occupies the position. It's often when respect is confused with fear. Parents and teachers can easily pass on this mistake if they themselves use their position to maintain authority over children. This is usually why many of us spend the rest of our life overly revering authority. We become impressed by the 'position', which blocks our ability to relate assertively to the 'person'. The person is not the position. This inclination to revere, if not fear, the position of authority sabotages our own self-authority in our own life.

Being impressed by the character of another blocks the development of your own character.

Whatever qualities you see in another you already have within yourself, otherwise you could not recognize them. But the more you allow yourself to be impressed by 'the others' character attributes the less you develop them for your self, within your self, and the more you are suppressing your own potential. That's not to say you don't 'appreciate' the qualities of another's character. Appreciation is an act of giving from inside out, whereas being 'impressed by' is an act of taking from outside in.

Being impressed by the intellect of another blocks the empowerment of your own intellect.

Your intellect is like an 'inner eye' that needs to be clear and free in order to focus and discern. But if you are always watching others and allowing their intellectual ability to impress you, it's as if the attention of your inner eye is 'caught' by them and is lost 'in' them. It is trapped in their intellectual capacity when you could be developing your own.

Being impressed by the achievements of others blocks your road to achievement.

When you raise someone else up on a pedestal on account of their achievements, and keep them there while talking about how impressed you are with them, you are likely to be subtly comparing your self to them. You will likely think and may even say, "I am not as good as them, and likely never will be as successful, as they are". In your consciousness you are using 'them' to suppress your self.

Being impressed by the belief systems, presented as truths by others, blocks your ability to discern what is true for you.

Even though what others are saying may 'ring true', if you don't 'realize' those truths for your self then just believing the beliefs of others will not empower you. In fact it is a sign of laziness when we cease to do the inner work of seeing and realizing what is true for ourselves. History reminds us what can happen when large numbers of people are impressed by one person and then follow that person out of 'blind belief'. They are so impressed it makes them so blind they cannot see the edge of the cliff!

Being continuously impressed by someone or some thing usually means we are using them to fill an illusory gap or hole in ourselves. This is hard to see until we step away and reflect on our own inner mental and intellectual processes. It is not saying don't appreciate the achievements or the talents of others. It's not saying don't acknowledge others qualities of character. But acknowledging and appreciating are not the same as 'being impressed by'.

When you are impressed you are subtly bowing, not out of humility, but more out of subservience. You are saying, albeit subtly or subconsciously, "You are greater, you are better, I am a lesser being". In such moments you are suppressing your self-esteem, self-respect and ultimately your self-confidence.

The difference between being impressed then getting lost in what you are impressed by, and being appreciative, can be seen in the theatre audience. Some people are so impressed by the performance they clap furiously and excitedly, perhaps even saying, "Weren't they just wonderful, marvelous, fantastic, I can't wait to come again". They are 'taking from' the performance. Whereas other people are quietly applauding as they 'give' their appreciation for the excellence of performance. They don't get excited about it all. They are 'giving to' the performers.

There is also an interesting paradox in all this. The less impressed *by* others you are the less you will want to make an impression *on* others yourself, in order to get their approval, the more you will naturally attract the appreciation *of* others.

Experiment and see for your self!

Question:
Who in life now or in the past has been the person/s that you have been
impressed by for longer than a few moments?

Reflection:
What do you think AND feel when you are 'impressed' by 'them'?

Action:
Experiment with transforming your energy towards them from
'being impressed by' into extending 'appreciation for'.

The Oxymorons of Life?

Have you ever noticed a blind spot in your eyesight? Often called a 'scotoma', it seems we all have one in at least one of our eyes. But we don't notice it as the other eye compensates and fills in the missing part of the picture! But have you spotted the blind spot in your inner eye, in what you might call your inner vision or awareness.

Most people are unaware of their physical 'scotoma' but some people set out to become fully aware of the blind spots in the inner eye. They realize they are often not 'seeing' i.e. understanding, something clearly and they know it is a form of internal blindness that is affecting their awareness in that moment.

A blind spot in your inner 'eye of awareness', often referred to as the eye of the intellect, or third eye, usually has one of three symptoms:

a) when you say one thing and do another and you are not aware of your own contradiction

b) when you 'accuse' others of a behavior that you are doing your self

c) when you hold on to a belief (usually subconsciously) which you know deep down is not true

Popular Contradictions

Such contradictions can come in many forms. When you criticize someone for always being critical and negative about things, you don't recognize that you are being critically negative about the criticizer! When you accuse others of being abusive you don't notice you are being abusive towards the abuser. When you hate the haters you can't see in that moment you have become the hater! When you tell someone you love them and then, a few moments or a few days later, become angry and blame them for what you feel, you are not aware you have just contradicted what you said. But, if challenged, you will likely justify your anger in the name of love by quoting one of the most popular musical oxymorons, namely 'love hurts'!

For some, such moments of contradiction can be frequent within an average day, but they will not be aware of it, not realize it, at the time. For others there is a feeling of discomfort that follows such contradictory perceptions, statements or actions, but they can't quite put their finger on why the discomfort arises. More often it is friends, family or colleagues who will point out our 'behavioral scotomas' allowing us to realize what we are not seeing for our self.

"You will likely justify your anger in the name of love by quoting one of the most popular oxymorons namely 'love hurts'."

Communal and collective contradictions can also be found in every day conversations. These are the many oxymorons that inhabit the landscapes of our consciousness, come through in our language and therefore shape our cultures. See if you can spot how many oxymorons are in the following passage.

She returned from a working holiday to find her son had being doing nothing most of the time except playing computer games based on virtual reality. Her husband was conspicuously absent so she called the agent to ask them for an accurate estimate on the value of her house. And while the agent was awfully nice and said that some aspects of the house looked better than new the local film production company had called and wanted it as a location for a black comedy about the living dead.

Managing Nothing

Other more commonly held contradictions become blind spots that can keep us collectively stuck in a kind of delusion. One of the most common examples is the idea of **'stress management'**. In the last twenty years a booming industry has arisen around this oxymoron and many have jumped on a bandwagon that is heading in a direction that doesn't help. I rode that wagon myself for some years until I spotted the oxymoron.

"Anger Management is another oxymoron, which sustains the illusion that anger can and should be managed."

Stress levels are frequently reported to be rising almost daily. Usually accompanied by doom-laden forecasts of collapsing health services and much corporate pain in the bottom line! There has been an explosion of panaceas that are often as varied as they are eccentric. All promising reliable ways to 'manage' your stress. But few have spotted the oxymoron. It is a classic contradiction in terms. When you are stressed you cannot manage anything, especially the stress itself. The stress is managing you! And who would want to 'manage' stress anyway?

Be free from stress, yes, manage stress, no!

The irony that lives in the very idea of stress management is that stress arises mainly because we are trying to control (manage) what we can never control, usually events and other people. So the only way out and into a stress free life is to stop trying to control (manage) what you cannot control, which is everything except your own thoughts about what you are trying to control! And you won't be able to control your thoughts if you are stressed, because your stress is essentially uncontrollable, negative thinking. An oxymoron and a paradox arriving together!

Anger Management is the same, another oxymoron, which sustains the illusion that anger can and should be managed.

Emotional Flood

One of the hot topics of the last decade has been 'emotional intelligence'. But few have realized it's also an oxymoron. When you are emotional you cannot be intelligent. A simple definition of intelligence is *'to use what you know in the right way in the right place at the right moment'*. Yet we all know from experience that when we become emotional the last thing we are able to do is calmly draw on our inner wisdom, create rational thoughts and clearly discern what is the appropriate response. When emotion floods through our consciousness it destroys our ability to act intelligently hence the sage advice to never make a life changing decision when you are emotional.

History is littered with the most obvious oxymoron in the idea of a **'holy war'**. To justify war by calling it a holy act looks like total blindness to the enlightened soul. Holy means sacred or approaching the divine, and war means almost the exact opposite. It is a violent and murderous exercise. We miss this most obvious of blind spots when we justify the use of war to create a pathway to the creation of peace. We have to 'fight for peace' is more than a slight contradiction. We are really saying we have to use violence to achieve non-violence. Few people have had the courage to 'flag up' such an obvious oxymoron; fewer have had the courage to listen and even fewer the courage to live the other way. Gandhi was perhaps one of the very few.

Justified Attack

On a more personal level, and sometimes a precursor to conflict, is another more common oxymoron in the form of **'constructive**

criticism' "I was only being constructive", says the criticizer, just after they have attacked the efforts, the ideas or the integrity of the other. To criticize is to attack and to attack anything or anyone can never be constructive. While the art, literature and drama critic has the job to 'critique', it is more like a review, unless and until emotion enters the review, then it becomes a personal reaction as opposed to a reflective response. Emotional projection is often the first sign of attack.

Perhaps one of the most public oxymorons is embedded in the title of one of our most prestigious global organizations known as the **United Nations.** The very fact we have separate national identities means real unity will always be impossible, which is quite plain to see in the reality of today's inter-nation relationships! Unity is only present when separation is absent. The title of the organization sustains the opposite of its mission. It's like saying 'we are all one'. Inherent in the 'we' is more than one, obviously!

"Our academic education is called learning but it's mostly memorizing, which is not learning, it's memorizing."

One oxymoron that influences us all is the idea of **'academic learning'.** Our academic education is called learning but its mostly memorizing, which is not learning, it's memorizing. It's also the memorization of other people's previous memorizations; people who are positioned as authority figures of the past. Their ideas are held in the highest esteem and passed on as 'authority'.

But real learning can only happen when the 'self' recognizes their self as their own authority in the universe of their own consciousness. Only then is real learning possible, which is learning what the self is and how the self works, how the self relates to other selves, how the self creates their world and why the self is here in the first place!

These aspects of the richness and capacity of 'the self' cannot be learned by a process of memorization of information. They are realized only through introversion and reflection, meditation and contemplation. If there is one subject in life that can never be 'academic' it is that of consciousness, which is 'the self' itself!

It is always an interesting exercise to watch out for the oxymorons that have become inherent within our cultures. They can easily influence your intentions and relationships. Hunting down your contradictions is very much a part of awakening and expanding your self-awareness. When you expose them within your consciousness you are shedding light on an illusion, exposing a delusion, and laying bare the truth. Such moments of enlightenment are grist to the mill of the spiritual traveler and vital steps to liberation in life.

Mmm...'spiritual traveler'... another oxymoron?

Question:
Have you ever realized you were contradicting your self or
doing something that contradicted something you said?
What was that action and do you still do it?

Reflection:
Why do we still find it hard to see the contradictions
that creep into our own life?

Action:
Create a conversation with friends or colleagues this week with
the purpose of identifying anything contradictory within
your actions and interactions as a group

(There were 9 oxymorons in the italicized paragraph)

Have YOU Lost the Plot?

One of the most common metaphors to describe life on earth is the idea of a 'drama' or in more contemporary terms, a movie. Shakespeare reminded us of the idea that the world is a just one big stage and suggested that we spend our life playing many roles. We tend not to see ourselves as actors, with options on many roles. Instead, we tend to identify with one or two fixed roles in our own private dramas. One at work and one at home. Then we make the common mistake of 'identifying' with the roles not realizing how this limits both our potential and our creative possibilities, resulting in our taking life far too seriously!

To learn to believe that you are the roles you play is to be asleep and unaware of how to live creatively and joyfully!

When we remind ourselves that we have both the opportunity to 'play' many roles AND also 'create' those roles, suddenly life starts to become creative and playful again! The mindset, and the consequent attitudes and behaviors, based on life as a creative and playful game would have been a reality in our childhood years. That's when many of us last 'played' for the sake of playing and we 'created' for the sake of creating.

Unfortunately such a joyfully creative approach is gradually suppressed by societies conditioning as we grow into the conventions of adult relationships, career paths and a sense of security that is based on the external material aspects of life. We easily learn to believe that the world is a dark and dangerous place, and start to perceive events and circumstances as threatening. We forget that we live in what is essentially an adventure playground where every scene and situation is an opportunity to play.

If we can see life more as a drama, as an opportunity to create and play as many roles as we want, we might also see that we can write our own script. It begins in our own heads where we populate our inner world with many characters and assign various roles to our self. We are all the masters of our own mental dramas and we are brilliant actors in our own minds. But when it comes to bringing our inner production, our roles, to life we find it difficult to 'act out'.

For many, if not most, it seems hard to actually 'realize' in real life the roles we might 'idealize' in our own minds.

The Adventures of YOU

Let's say for a moment you believed that you really could write the story of your life. Once written, you will also be the producer, director and star in **The Adventures of ME**. How would you like it to be? How would you see your life story unfolding? All good stories start with an idea, a concept, and an outline! It is reckoned that all stories with a beginning, middle and end, especially in 'Holywoodland', will fall into one of seven possible categories or themes. In the spirit of creativity, which 'theme' best describes The Adventures of ME as you might creatively envision it?

1 Your Life as a Tale of RAGS TO RICHES

This is the story of an ordinary person who finds a second more exceptional self within. Examples might include Cinderella, Great Expectations and My Fair Lady. During a process of transformation a naturally beautiful character is rediscovered within and emerges as the story unfolds. Can you see how your life may be a transformational process, a story of redemption, as you rediscover your true, powerful character and the wealth of your spirit, that's you, within?

2 Your Life as THE QUEST

This is the long and hazardous journey to reach a priceless goal far away. Examples include The Odyssey, Jason and the Golden Fleece and Raiders of the Lost Ark. Are you currently on a quest? Reading this book probably indicates that you are to some extent. You are hunting the truth about life, the true purpose of life, truly how life should be lived. Inevitably there are obstacles both outside and in! You will find your golden fleece!

3 Your Life as a Tale of VOYAGE AND RETURN

This is the story in which some event – a fall, crash or shipwreck – propels the hero or heroine out of their familiar surroundings into a disconcerting and abnormal world in which they eventually prevail. Alice in Wonderland and Robinson Crusoe are perfect examples. Do you sense you have fallen? Have you had your 'brick wall' moment, your dark night of the soul period? Are you in it right now? Are you set to prevail? Are you sensing you are ready to emerge victorious?

4 Your Life as a COMEDY

This is a story that highlights the odd, the absurd and the innocent mistakes of the main character. Tom Jones, Faulty Towers and Some Like it Hot are perfect examples. Sometimes we can only laugh at our life and how it has, and is, unfolding. That laughter in itself then draws to us people and situations that reflect and empower the lightness of our being.

5 Your Life as a TRAGEDY

This is the archetypal plot with a five-stage structure culminating in destruction and death. The main character is overcome by a desire for power/passion, which either destroys them or they become monstrous. Macbeth, Lolita and King Lear are classic examples. Perhaps not the most joyful way to create our life but it seems many of us will be the central character in our own self-created tragedies, until we learn certain lessons, change certain mindsets and thereby rise again like the phoenix from the ashes!

6 Your Life as a Tale of REBIRTH

Someone falls under a dark power or a spell that traps him or her in a state of living death. A miraculous act of redemption takes place and the victim is released and brought into the light. Classic examples include Sleeping Beauty, a Christmas Carol and the Sound of Music. In many ways we are all living in an era of darkness in what is now an increasingly violent world. It's not difficult to join in and even add to that darkness with our own endarkened state of mind. Until it's obvious we cannot tolerate it any more and something or someone triggers in us an awakening to an alternative and almost opposite way to live. We are then awakened to our true self. Our enlightenment is a kind of rebirth, which sets us free to return to our natural joyful state.

7 Your Life as a Tale of OVERCOMING THE MONSTER

A hero or heroine confronts the monster, defeats it against all odds and wins the treasure or a loved ones hand. David and Goliath, Dracula and JAWS fit this profile. One of the monsters we all share is our continuous consumption of the world. When we consume the world it eventually consumes us as we become dependent and addicted to something, someone, somewhere etc. This monster is defeated when we learn to live with simplicity and gentleness, with compassion and kindness.

Which Theme Will You Choose?

If you do sit down and start to write the script of your life you would probably notice that each theme is connected to the others. It would be tempting, if not impossible, to include a mix of all the themes. Your creativity would probably include a taste of each, if only because that would be more fun. The honesty of your creation would probably also oblige you to include some threads from each. Even more 'interestingly', if you did consciously set out on any authentic spiritual path you will be choosing, albeit unknowingly at first, to write, produce, direct and enact all seven themes at some stage on that path. To complete your journey you would not be able to avoid them! But you would probably only realize that on arrival!

So Let Us Begin

From a purely spiritual point of view the **QUEST** is possibly the best metaphor for the spiritual journey. It is a journey in which we search for that priceless goal, which is the realization of ones true self after a lifetime (some might say several lifetimes) of ignorance of our true self. Everyone is 'questing', which really means searching in some way or other for their own authenticity. But it seems only a few realize they are only and always looking for themselves. Even fewer 'get' that they are looking in the wrong direction.

"Only the 'kiss of truth', which is the realization of who you really are as an ageless spiritual being, can fully re-awaken you!"

In your spiritual QUEST for the holy grail of truth and happiness your **VOYAGE AND RETURN** will propel you into the strange and unfamiliar territory of your own consciousness. There you will notice the presence of paradox, contradiction and ambiguity. What you previously thought were the certainties of life turn out to be little more than a morning mist that evaporates it the first hint of the sun. One the most disconcerting and disorienting insights is the fact that you are actually the creator of your drama, your primary reality is within your own consciousness, and not 'out there' in what we all agree to call 'the world'. This one insight alone, the result of a 'voyage' within, can empower you to 'return' to living a whole new way life.

The Kiss of Truth

Eventually The Adventures of You will become a tale of **REBIRTH** as you realize that you have slipped into a deep slumber induced by the spell of many illusions (false beliefs). You fell asleep which, in spiritual terms, means the loss of true self-awareness and the awareness of what is true. You were lulled into your self-forgetful state by the sleepiness i.e. the unawareness of those around you. Your spiritual beauty has therefore lain dormant, unrevealed and suppressed by the 'belief' that you are only an aging and decaying physical form, trying to survive in a dangerous world. Having surrendered to this state of sleepiness only the 'kiss of truth', which is the realization of who you really are as an ageless spiritual being, can fully re-awaken your powerful, beautiful and creative self.

As you increase your awakened state you realize there is only one **MONSTER** of the deep, and that is your own subconscious. It is in your subconscious that you have been accumulating and storing dark, distorted, illusory images of your self and stories about your self. A battle with the monster may commence and continue for some time, until you realize it's a battle with what is not real. You are not the stories that you have previously created and told about your self. You are not a story! Then, one day, you see the MONSTER for what it truly is, a ghost with many heads. But it ceases to scare you as you realize ghosts have no substance. To ignore it is to kill it.

Happy Endings
Along the way there has to be a sense of **TRAGEDY** because destruction and death is necessary. Loss is inevitable until it is seen for what it is, another illusion!

There will be the destruction of the old habits and behaviors that have kept you trapped in your own suffering. Then there is the death and loss of all the old false identities that have been sustaining those old behaviors. There will be the disappearance of all accumulated dependencies as all the stories that have been built around those dependencies collapse. All this death and destruction, release and disappearance, will feel, at times, more than a little 'tragic', until **REBIRTH** is complete and reality is restored.

Only then can YOU reinstate your self to your true position as the master of your own consciousness. Only then can you restore the real spiritual power that you need to create a benevolent life and a happy ending to your script. (If indeed there is such a thing as an ending!)

Laughter Therapy

And yet there must inevitably be moments of laughter as you frequently realize this whole 'life and living thing' is simply a divine **COMEDY**. You have been taking 'it all' far too seriously. What you believed was real and true now seems absurd and crazy e.g. the idea that others are responsible for your happiness becomes simply illogical, the idea that success in life is just getting a promotion at work becomes ridiculous, the idea that true love in life can 'only' be found with one other special person becomes nonsensical!

"You are not the stories that you have previously created and told about your self."

They are just some of the many illusions that are now so obviously...illusions! The realization that life has no purpose, other than to live, leaves you with a smile in your heart, a sparkle in your eye and a laughter that is highly infectious. What else can you do but laugh when you realize how complex and difficult you tried to make it and how utterly simple it all really is.

And then, when the **QUEST** is nearing its end it will become obvious you have starred in your own created tale of RAGS to RICHES. While you used to think you had some riches in the material world, you now see they were just rags to the spirit you now know you are. You rediscover your real wealth in the form of the love that you emanate, the compassion that you disseminate, the contentment that you radiate, the truth that you demonstrate and the joy that you exude!

They are the true riches of spirit, which are available in abundance on the inside. But the plot, like all good plots, has one final twist. They are riches that can only be known and sustained in abundance when they are shared!

Question:
Which of the above 'themes' do you think you are
presently going through in your life?

Reflection:
Why do you think you often tend to take life far too seriously?

Action:
Make a list of all the roles that you think you are playing in your life at the
moment. Then make another list of all the roles you could possibly play.
Then contemplate both lists and write down
what they say to you about you.

Simply Patience

Have you ever played a waiting game? People sometimes do it within intimate relationships, as they wait for the other to commit! Teams sometimes do it during periods of the 'game' as they wait for the opening that allows them to create an advantage. Parents sometimes do it as they await the full potential of their children to flower. Bird watchers definitely do it as they lie in wait for a rare sight of a feathered friend!

Have you ever consciously decided not to hurry something, somehow knowing, deep within, that everything will happen in the right way at the right time? The older and mellower amongst us tend to do this as there grows, with time, a more accurate intuition about what will be! Have you ever decided not to rush somewhere realizing you cannot make yourself arrive faster than your mode of transport, and you cannot control what gets in the way? Bus drivers learn to do it. Even in the midst of a Grand Prix, believe it or not, racing drivers have to do it. Patience is relative!

Patience is one of those virtues that can transform a moment of high anxiety into quiet relaxation, a rush of mental agitation into the smooth flowing river that life can be. In the presence of a patient person we are surrounded by an aura of calm. We are pulled into the tranquil light of their unhurriedness. Even when they are busy, the 'quality' of their busy-ness still radiates patience. Perhaps they heard Emerson's advice to, "Adopt the pace of nature: her secret is patience". Nature is always 'patiently busy', visibly or invisibly.

In a recent survey by a national newspaper they set out to discover why levels of anger were rising in the world. They found that the most frequent underlying cause was that people's expectations and desires were not fulfilled... fast enough! In other words, impatience with events, with governments, with other people and with delivery services, are the new variants of 'hurry sickness'.

Perhaps it's not surprising, considering the speed of modern life. The email addict, the Facebook fixated, the tense texter and the tweeting twitterer, are almost always impatiently looking for the next opportunity to get online, access their inbox and make chattering noises!

"The email addict, the fixated facebooker, the tense texter and the tweeting twitterer, are almost always impatiently looking for the next opportunity to get online and start to make chattering noises!"

While most people might admit to being impatient in some area of their life, not many know how to free themselves from the quickening anxieties that signify impatience is 'inbound'! Many, if not most, would probably say that they would rather not be so impatient, that they do want to be more patient, but the only problem is, they want it now! Obviously restoring a little more patience to your life will require some... patience!

So how can you be more patient? Can you, with one thought, decide to become a patient person? Can patience be a permanent thread woven through your personality? How do you create patience?

Begin with VISUALIZATION
Being patient is a creative process. It involves bringing together a variety of ingredients in an initial process of visualization. The first

step is to admit and acknowledge the 'impatient trait' in your character is entirely your own creation. It's not the late train or failing delivery service, it's you that makes you impatient. You have created and sustained the 'trait' of impatience, so you are capable of creating and sustaining patience. Like all your other creations the process begins on the screen of your mind. This is where you conceive, believe and achieve patience 'in rehearsal', before you step out onto the stage and 'do it' in daily life. This is where you complete the creative process from idea to image to feeling to action. To do that, you will need to draw on a variety of inner ingredients.

Access a Little PEACE

The first resource is a 'felt inner peace'. This is the peace of your heart, the peace that can never be taken from you, but which you do lose awareness of. Like the 'foundation layer' some will put on their face in the morning, peace is the foundation energy of patience! If you cannot draw on the power of your inner peace, patience will be almost impossible. Meditation is the journey of no distance in one second into your spiritual heart (the heart of your consciousness) where you will always find an unlimited supply of pure peace.

Add a Quiet ACCEPTANCE

Your inner peace can only travel from your heart to your mind when you no longer want to change what is. The moment you accept everyone and everything as you find them, without any resistance, is the moment the power of love, your love, that's YOU, are able to embrace life in its totality, as it is. That alone is quite a challenge for many of us as we have a tendency to spend too much time and energy not in our hearts, but in our minds. That's where we 'judge' others and 'fix' the problems of the world, under the illusion that it's our job, and that we can! From this mental habit comes not acceptance but resistance. And resistance is not a building block of patience.

Your inner peace, and your acceptance of what is, are like two primary colors which, when mixed together, create contentment. You cannot be patient unless you are content in your self, with your self and with the world, in this moment now. This also requires the realization that there is only 'now'. Only then will all attempts to escape into the future or hide in the past, come to an end.

Drizzle with FAITH

Only within this still, quiet, yet dynamic state of contentment, which is not passive or submissive, but alert and available, can you hear and feel the wisdom that comes from the truth that you already hold deep in your heart. Intuitively you now know all is well and all will be well. Your faith in life emerges as an intuitive knowingness that, in the words of that now famous and well circulated text called Desiderata, "all is unfolding exactly as it should". With your faith in life restored, your most frequent thought is 'what's the hurry'!

Flavor with FREEDOM

Only once you are at peace, exercising acceptance, contented, and with a faith that life is always unfolding as it should, can you 'see' and realize you no longer need to 'acquire anything' from outside your self. This signals the end of all desire, the death of craving and the atrophy of dependency. Nothing need be sought, for everything needed is already present within the self. While our body has needs, ultimately you, the self, doesn't. The key word here is 'ultimately'. On the way to freedom from all neediness you need to increase your self-awareness until you are completely... self-aware! Then, any residual neediness permanently disappears. Until this distinction, between physical form that you occupy and the energy of the conscious self that you are, is clear, impatience will continue to show up.

But in the moment you realize you already have all that you seek within. In the moment you realize you have been searching in the wrong place for what you already have. In the moment you realize that the peace and happiness you seek are not 'out there' and therefore can never be delivered 'on time', all impatience is seen for what it is, the result of a temporary lack of self awareness.

Once self-awareness is restored there re-emerges, from inside out, an intuitive faith and confidence that life will show up with exactly what your body needs, when it needs it, to simply live and live simply. You are then free, you feel free and you live freely from the heart. Making it impossible to create thoughts of impatience.

Allow to Rise with Pure INTENTION

The realization of this, the deepest freedom, the freedom of the spirit that we are, signals the end of the slavery to 'wanting' and there follows a natural transformation of intention. You now know all that 'you' ever needed was and is already within you. Life ceases to be about waiting impatiently for what you want or expect, and starts to be focused around giving what you have. Every moment is seen as an opportunity to be 'the giver' of the energy of your life. Not as a sacrifice or as an obligation, or a duty, but as a gift. Time, attention, guidance, warmth, acceptance and many other forms of the energy of you, all become the real gifts, the true gifts, which require no expenditure, no packaging and no transportation.

Impatience is a sign that we are 'not well' in our being. It makes us 'a patient' requiring treatment. It means one of the above active ingredients is temporarily missing, probably suppressed. That's why life is a healing process until your patience is restored and is expressed by the simplicity with which you live your life. Each moment you attempt to force an outcome, each moment of anxious waiting or expectant desire, is simply deepening a wound in your being that will eventually require the balm of peace, the acceptance that comes from love and the realization of the self as a spiritual being free of all dependency.

Don't Just Do Something!

Perhaps the most valuable application of the virtue of patience is its ability to invite wisdom back to life. In most western cultures, when things appear to be going wrong, we have the tendency to shout, "Don't just sit there, DO something!" Whereas, in the ancient and wiser east there was the tendency to whisper, "Don't just do something, SIT there." In such moments we acknowledge the need to patiently allow a deeper wisdom to inform the creation of our responses, and not allow a knee jerk emotional reaction to rule our mind and heart.

Wisdom however, does not appear in the auditorium of our consciousness on demand. An invitation must be sent to our heart, and then a patient wait is often required before a reply is received. Perhaps this is why the wise and the patient know that patience and wisdom are inseparable companions.

Perhaps this is why the farmer's wisdom is patience itself, and the gardener's patience is wisdom itself.

Question:
In what areas of your life are you currently impatient and why?

Reflection:
Which of the above seven ingredients of patience do you think you are missing most (rate each on a scale of one to ten).

Action:
Take each one of the above on separate day during this coming week and contemplate it, reflect on it, explore its meaning and see what it awakens, shifts and heals within you

The Anatomy of an Argument

A few decades ago the world famous comedians from Monty Pythons Flying Circus created what became one of their funniest sketches. The Argument Clinic was based around the idea of 'buying an argument' from someone in the 'argument room', whose first question was, "Would you like the five minute argument or the ten minute argument sir?"

It seems many people grew up in a context where arguing was a regular feature of family life. It was there that they developed their inclination to argue. For the rest of their life they would often find themselves, both consciously and subconsciously, looking for an argument. Although they have no negative motive (it's just a habit) others do get bored and sometimes irritated with what has become their argumentative nature.

Armed with Opinion

However, there are those who are always looking to pick a verbal fight. They deliberately look for someone to disagree with, so they can build an emotional 'head of steam' and proceed to re-create and vent their frustrations and angers. They become 'argument addicts' as the emotion also gives them a physical buzz. Some of us are way down the other end of the spectrum and we instantly shy away from any kind of verbal confrontation. Most of us are probably somewhere between the two. A few have realized the futility of any kind of argument because they understand the 'anatomy of an argument'.

Do you ever argue? When you argue it means you have an opinion, and at the heart of your opinion is your belief. When you hear the belief of the other you argue back because you are seeing their belief as a threat to you personally. Why, because you are attached to, and identified with, your belief. So you interpret the other's belief as a personal attack. Before you know it you are either defending or attacking, which means you are creating both fear and anger, which expresses as aggression, which means you are inflicting emotional suffering upon your self.

Face Saving

Many people come to a conversation 'armed' with their opinions, prepared to defend their beliefs, and ready to do battle. It's easy to disarm them. All you have to say is, "That's an interesting way to

"There are those who deliberately look for an argument; they are spoiling for a fight so they can satisfy their addiction to the accompanying emotions."

see it. I'm not sure I agree with it, but I can appreciate you have your point of view". If we find this hard to do it's because we believe we are right, and we want to prove we are right and they are wrong. Why, because when we are right we are happy! Being right we feel superior and feeling superior is the best way to avoid the possibility of feeling inferior! So being right, being superior and being happy become synonymous. But it's obviously not true happiness because in the process of attempting to prove our rightness we are tense and even angry that the other is not 'getting it' or that they are not acknowledging that 'I am right'. The possibility of losing the argument becomes the possibility of losing face.

Emotional Addiction

Then there are those who deliberately look for an argument regardless of who is right or wrong. They are spoiling for a fight so they can satisfy and justify their addiction to the accompanying emotions i.e. anxiety, anger and perhaps hate. Like hard drugs, if these emotions are indulged in, they will have to be 'felt' every day, hence the continuously 'argumentative attitude' that some develop. They are effectively saying, " Go on, I dare you to disagree with me", which is another way of saying, "Go on, press my buttons, make my day"!

But it's good to have an opinion isn't it? If you don't have an opinion about important issues you will be seen as weak, right? And if you don't stand up and fight for the rightness of your opinion you may be accused of being soft, conciliatory, without the courage of your convictions, yes? This is how some people often justify holding an opinion about anything and everything. But wait a second – in the moment of expressing your opinion, if it is in the defense of a position or designed to be against another opinion, it is therefore the birthplace of conflict and the seed of war.

Origins of War

All wars, at their roots, are just differences of opinion, a clash of beliefs. The emotions and actions that follow are primarily a violence upon oneself. Then they emerge as violent behaviors towards others. The truth of this is then avoided with the claim, "We had to be strong to make the decision to go to war", which is really a way of avoiding saying, "We weren't strong enough to 'let go' of our need to be right", and "We didn't have the courage or the patience to turn an argument into a dialogue"... where the first principle of dialogue is always the intention to truly understand the others position and therefore the others point of view.

It takes wisdom to have a point of view, and yet be extremely interested in others points of view, to the extent that we are prepared to shift your viewing point! This says, "I am flexible and I acknowledge there are many ways of looking and seeing this issue". It says, "I have the humility to learn from you", and it says, "**I seek to meet you on the ground we share, as opposed to fight you from a proclaimed territory.**"

The Arithmetic of an Argument

What's the difference between a discussion, a dialogue and an argument? In essence, a discussion is an open exchange of views, a dialogue is a mutual exploration of meaning and an argument is a battle of opinions. An argument is the meeting of two closed minds. A discussion is only possible when we are open to one another's ideas. A dialogue will only happen when two parties collaborate to uncover a deeper wisdom and co-create a new understanding.

"A dialogue is a mutual exploration of meaning, a discussion is an open exchange of views and an argument is a battle of opinions."

In an argument 1 + 1 = nothing. In a discussion 1 + 1 = 2. In a dialogue 1 + 1 = 3. In a dialogue there is more listening than talking. In a discussion there is an equal exchange between friends. In an argument there is war! It is an enlightened soul that leads the conversation from an argument to a discussion to a dialogue, a process that is driven not by the need to be right, but by a genuine curiosity, alongside the intention to understand and learn from the other. The presence of curiosity is a usually a good sign of the absence of the ego that wants to be right all the time.

One day three pupils came to see their master. The master held up a flower and asked his pupils what color they saw. The first pupil said, "A reddish brown". And the master said, "You are right". The second pupil said, "I see a bluish purple color" And the master said, "You are right". To which the third pupil said, "But master, both cannot be right". To which the master replied, "You are right"!

When we realize that everyone sees everything from a different point of view it's possible to realize there is no right or wrong. Yes, in the context of some issues, there will be some perceptions and interpretations that may be more 'accurate' than others. But ultimately, to an enlightened soul, there is no right or wrong, just an infinite variety of perceptions.

Question:

Who do you find yourself arguing with most, either verbally or mentally,
and what do you argue about, and why are
you really arguing with them...really?

Reflection:

Imagine yourself exchanging ideas with that person where you are doing
most of the listening and, at the end of which you let them
have the last word. How might the conversation sound?

Action:

Practise creating a dialogue with one other person this week. Pick a person
pick a topic, pick a place to meet, pick three questions
around that topic and then pick each others
brains in a free flowing mutual enquiry.

You can view the Monty Python 'Argument Clinic' at
http://www.youtube.com/watch?v=teMlv3ripSM

The Power of Your Presence

Are you present or do you just have presence? While they are connected there is a difference between being 'present' and the power of 'presence'. Being present is to be aware of your self being aware of the here and now, often referred to as 'present moment awareness'.

PRESENCE however is what others feel when they notice your proximity without vocal or visible cues. Everyone carries and communicates a certain 'presence' wherever they are, whoever they are and into whatever they are doing. The 'presence' of some is so powerful it seems able to touch and influence almost everyone in their vicinity. And yet the 'presence' of others seems to have no influential effect, to such an extent they are almost completely ignored by others, even when they speak! Most of us probably fall somewhere between these two extremes.

So what is 'presence' exactly? Can it be manufactured, cultivated and even magnified? Why would you want to and what difference would it make?

Someone 'has presence' when our attention is drawn to them for no apparent reason. It is a form of subtle attraction that doesn't have an obvious cause. It has nothing to do with appearances. But before understanding the true nature of presence it's perhaps useful to eliminate the kinds of presence that are not so present...so to speak!

Types of Presence

Often, in a group or a meeting, there is the **QUIET ONE**, often called the 'silent type'. After a while their quiet and yet seemingly attentive non-participation attracts the attention of others. They can seem to be using the power of their silent presence so that others will draw them into the conversation. And yet, if they say something that is irrelevant, or even inappropriate, it may become obvious they are probably just shy. Which is not presence, just fear!

Then there is what we could be called **CELEBRITY PRESENCE**. Someone with a claim to public fame will always have some mystique surrounding them, which is often just a sense of awe that is projected on to them by others. But this is not real presence, it's more likely a combination of the mystery of the real person behind a public persona and the privilege of a much talked about person

> *"Everyone carries and communicates a certain 'presence' wherever they are, whoever they are and into whatever they are doing."*

'appearing live' in a space near you! And yet some of 'the famous' do seem to have an authentic and powerful attraction that emanates from a deeper place than reputation or appearances. They do have 'presence' and they need to say or do very little to have a significant influence upon those around them.

Then there is the presence of the **HERO** who's reputation, usually based on some great deed of derring-do, goes before them. This kind of presence tends to inspire a genuine respect and an implicit affirmation that their greatness is much greater than our own greatness could ever be. Yet there is probably an element of awe inspired deference, or perhaps even worship, at work. The presence of the hero can be an inspiration but it tends to wane fast once they become absent from our view and/or we seek new heroes.

Then there is the presence of **INNOCENCE**. Perhaps one of the most attractive attributes of a human being is a felt 'purity of innocence'. In a child or adult this innocence draws our attention and somehow we feel safe in their presence or moved by their presence or empowered through their presence. Yet it's impossible to pursue or manufacture innocence. Perhaps that's why it's so rare!

Then there is the presence of the **WISE ONE**. To sense we are in the presence of someone who has a wisdom beyond words is to become aware of a power that has the potential to move us to change our life. The presence of wisdom is usually accompanied by a combination of humility and clarity, depth and gentleness, ease and kindness. And yet, if we *"Real beauty however, at the deepest human level, is felt and known when we are touched by the beauty of another's being."* notice the slightest 'hurt pride' or any superiority or superficiality within our wise one's demeanor we quickly notice the power of their presence diminishing. Once again there is likely to be a fair amount of projection, especially if we harbor a subtle desire for them to be our savior and/or our guide.

The Beauty of Presence

Beauty has presence and, in some ways, it is presence. If there is a beautiful object in the room its beauty draws our attention towards itself. The beautiful appearance of a perfect human face and form will also turn heads and attract attention. Real beauty however, at the deepest human level, is felt and known when we are touched by the beauty of another's being. The fundamental characteristic of the power of presence that emanates from a beautiful being is 'radiance'; it is the radiant light of their consciousness.

The Light of Presence

As the light of a lamp radiates outwards to fill the room it will illuminate everything equally and entirely as long as there is nothing in the way. As soon as a lampshade is placed around the light, or objects are placed in the room, then the light will find obstacles to its radiant path. It will deviate and shadows will appear. Its brightness will be denied to many parts of the room.

And so it is with the radiant energy of a person whose 'presence' is felt. It is an invisible energy, a vibration that originates from their consciousness. Like all forms of light the light of consciousness is designed to radiate outwards, in all directions, away from its source. And when it does, fully unhindered and unblocked, it touches everything, which really means has the potential to influence everyone, in its path.

360 Degrees of Presence

When we are on the receiving end of the radiance of such an unhindered and therefore pure consciousness we 'feel' the vibration of that energy. Sometimes we call it love; sometimes we feel a deep and profound peace, sometimes a quiet joy. Depending on our receptivity we 'feel' the presence of the other. Like the filament in a light bulb, the light of consciousness radiates naturally 360 degrees. Unless there is something in the way! It's what's 'in the way' of the light of our consciousness, of our self, that defines the power and quality of our radiant energy. This in turn will define the range and effect of our personal presence.

> *"Instead of 'using' our mind we get 'lost in' our mind."*

So what diminishes the power of our radiance? What exactly dilutes the power of our, or anyone's, presence?

Living in the Mind

Essentially it's our mind, or more accurately, what we put on our mind and to what extent we get lost in what is on our mind. For each one of us the mind is the arena of creation. It's like an artist's canvas, a screen that we can use to generate ideas, images, concepts etc. We also use it to bring the world out there, in here! We use it to run old movies called memories. And it's into what is on our mind that we most frequently try to escape and thereby lose our light, our radiance, our presence. We become preoccupied.

When we go into what is on our mind it signals our absence! Instead of using our mind we get lost in our mind. It is in our mind that we become attached to ideas, images, memories etc. And any form of attachment means the energy of our self, our consciousness, is 'trapped in' and 'blocked by' what's on our mind. Sometimes we even sense when someone is lost in a mental story and we say to them, "Are you OK, I get the sense there's something on your mind".

It's only when someone is completely free within themselves that their 'presence' can be felt in all directions. They are fully present and the energy of their consciousness is radiating freely. They never attempt to 'escape' into something on their mind. That doesn't mean they are mindless, more likely they are masters of their mind, able to use this 'tool of creativity' accurately and when appropriate. They have a clear inner awareness of their self that is quite distinct from their mind.

They know that their mind is integral to their consciousness. They are aware that mental activity/creativity is like a 'computer programme' that can be summoned to put what we want on our computer screen with a click or a slide! In an instant up comes the programme on the screen that is required to perform a certain task. Similarly within the self, within our consciousness, we can summon up the 'screen of our mind' and use it to perform a specific task such as creating a vision, or creating a list of options to act, or juxtaposing two different ideas or concepts, or a visualization of the future etc. And then, when the task is finished, we can instantly dissolve the screen and send our mind into the background of our awareness

Running Our Stories

Unfortunately most of us don't learn how to do this. Instead we learn to keep many mental screens running in our consciousness and create the habit of jumping from one to the other. When we don't like one we jump into another without properly closing the previous screen, without ending and closing the previous story. Or if we like one we jump into it and start to live through it, rather like watching a movie at the cinema. We get lost in the stories that we are running on what may be various mental screens.

"We get lost in the stories that we are running on what may be various mental screens."

Or we imagine something that we are watching on our mind is being threatened, so we create even more thoughts of anxiety and worry. Or we just keep running the world 'out there' on the screen of our mind 'in here' and then lose ourselves in the lives of others. All these become inner habits that distort, defocus and diminish the radiant power of our consciousness, our self, our being! This is what tends to dilute the power of our presence.

Then, whatever does radiate outwards is 'weak energy' carrying a weak vibration. Most common is the vibration of fear that is always based on a mental story of imagined future loss, or anger based on the mental story that someone else is to blame for what we feel, or sadness based on the mental story of some remembered loss. These vibrations of our consciousness are not the signs of a 'powerful presence' but the symptoms of a 'self' that is internally fragmented and somewhat lost in what's on their mind.

Undisturbable Easiness

This is probably why the most influential 'presence' comes from someone who is completely undistracted by anything external or internal. While they have a 'present moment' attentiveness and concentration, there is an obvious stillness of being. They have an inner freedom from all mental distraction or pre-occupation, and an undisturbable easiness that allows the emanation of the clearest radiant energy from their consciousness. Sometimes it's called the 'charisma of contentment'. They never 'react heatedly' and are always able to generate a calm and 'cool response'.

It appears that such a state of consciousness has the power to touch and therefore influence others well beyond the immediate vicinity and at the most subtle levels. It is also something we can all cultivate and experiment with, even in the midst of our daily distractions! In the process of developing the 'power of your presence' perhaps the efficacy of the following exercise is worth testing:

An Experiment

Visualize someone in your mind with whom you are currently having a difficult relationship. Don't run your 'relationship story' in your mind but consciously send them calm and loving good wishes through your mind. Two things happen which are outside the remit of any 'scientific enquiry'! First, 'they' receive that energy which carries a higher vibrational image of them than they have of themselves in the context of your relationship with them. This is uplifting and empowering for them.

Secondly you start to heal your previously dark image of them, which you have created in previous encounters. This is like clearing a dark mental cloud and is a form of self-healing, but that's another seminar!

Both these effects then bode well for the next actual real time face-to-face encounter with that person, making the connection and exchange of energy easier, lighter and more loving. Experiment and see if it works for you. If you can then expand this particular effect of your 'presence' in one particular relationship to a more unlimited benevolence towards all others, you may get some sense of the meaning of 360 degrees of presence. It is a state where everyone and all beings in all kingdoms are touched by the light of your consciousness radiating from your cleanest, clearest and most powerful state.

Yes it's true, it is probably also the consciousness of a saint or an angel, but then, aren't we all, in some sense, potential saints and angels. Aren't we all in training, right here in the big school we call life!

Question:
What stories do you tend to run in your mind that stops you from being fully present and therefore a powerful presence?

Reflection:
Who do you know that you believe has a 'certain presence' - what do you sense gives them this presence.

Action:
During the coming week use the above exercise in three 'challenging' relationships and see what a difference it makes.

Do YOU Sit in
the Seat of Stillness

Our towns and cities are loud with the sounds of perpetual endeavor. The car is much less a servant and more an addiction, technology is less a tool and more a tyrant, the clock is less a measure of time and more the master of our life. People rush from eating to meeting, from keyboard to console, from shop to cinema, with less time than ever to give to each other. Increasingly, we feel the urge to escape the pressures that seem to assail us.

But we tend to escape into more activity and noise that we believe will relax us, but more often only further distracts our mind and agitates our heart. There comes a point however, through the noise of complexity *"When you are in this state of stillness you naturally become aware of your timelessness, your eternity."* and complication, when we recognize an inner call that pulls us back towards simplicity. A feeling tugs our heart. At the core of this feeling is a power more magnetic than any industry can promise or any city life can offer – the simple healing power of silence.

Silence is that profound aspect of creation that evokes ideas of infinity, the grandeur of our spirit and the possibility of an authentic and deep personal peace.

Silence should never be regarded as merely nothingness or emptiness. It is the very ground of creation and the ultimate source of creativity. A composer knows that the silence behind and between the notes, are as much a part of the symphony as the notes themselves. The painter begins with both an empty canvas and a quiet mind. It is the unseen silence of the canvas that will hold the artists creative expression together. It is also an unseen and unfelt silence that holds together the canvas that is the multidimensional backdrop of all our daily lives. But we are far from being aware of it!

At the heart of the creative beings that we all are, there is a silent and still place from which all that we create arises. Just as the center of a wheel is still, just as the point on which the spinning top spins is still, and just as the nucleus of the atom, around which the electrons travel, is still, so the center of our being is completely still. Stillness is the core of every being. If that stillness was not real we would all go not so quietly insane!

No Movement No Change

Our life both emerges from and revolves around this still and silent point within the 'inner space' of our consciousness. When we are still we are as we originally were and always will be. No thing, just being. In that inner 'seat' there is no movement of thought or feeling, memory or belief. Where there is no movement there is no change, and where there is no change there is no time, only the timeless. When you are in this still state you become aware of your own timelessness, your own eternity.

It is 'here', which is nowhere, that you know the deepest peace, the peace of pure being. It is the most profound relaxation. In lives easily lived in the pursuit of 'more', this silent and still point will always signal you to return, to simply sit and be your 'self'... and nothing more! If you don't acknowledge and follow that signal it's fairly certain life will mysteriously arrange for something to ensure that you do!

Where are YOU Going?

Some say there is a spiritual journey to be made, a process of self transformation, a 'becoming', a movement from a self that is lost and trapped in a noisy and heated world, to a serene self that restores it's freedom from all the trials and travails of the world. Others say there is no journey because there is nowhere to go. They say that while human bodies may go from here to there, the human spirit, the self, goes

"The 'still point' that we are, the centeredness of our being, is never more than one second and no distance away."

nowhere, because there is only ever 'here'! They say there is only being, just being, and being is never there, only 'here'!

Bewitched and Bedazzled

They say that the being is never not being, it just 'seems' otherwise. And that 'seeming otherwise' happens when we 'apparently' leave the core of our being, where we know exactly who we are, and start creating the belief/s that we are something 'other'! We start believing we are our form and personality. And when we 'believe' we are just the form that we occupy we are bewitched and bedazzled by a form filled world. We travel across horizontal planes, driven by a variety of machines, searching in a thousand other forms for the holy grail of happiness.

When we believe we are just a personality we aspire to travel in vertical planes, driving by a vehicle called ambition, in search of the elevation that will signify success. In the process we create noise and heat, agitation and frustration. And they are only tiring. The more we attempt to travel both horizontally and vertically, in the world of forms, the further we seem from the place of coolness and peace that is the silence and stillness of the heart of our being. Yet we will pine for that place, for that inner space, without knowing it.

No one is able to tell us that the 'still point' that we are, is never more than one second and no distance away. Even fewer, it seems, can show us the way there!

When we do surrender to the 'call of the heart', being quiet and sitting in stillness puts the rushing world around us into a new perspective. It is seen for what it is, a gathering of creative beings who have mistakenly learned to believe that 'important' things must be done today in order to ensure tomorrow will be OK. Trapped in fearful attempts to 'secure the future' the power and the beauty of 'the moment' are missed. The present is not only lost, it is eventually avoided. We learn to live in a projected ideal of the future, and we miss the reality of now. Our peace seems lost, our love has disappeared and our happiness is perpetually delayed.

"When you realize you could not 'be' anywhere else you will smile the smile that arrives with a moment of enlightenment."

So how do you 'be' in this inner space? In truth the question is irrelevant because you are already there. And when you realize and recognize you could not 'be' anywhere else... you'll smile the smile that arrives with a moment of enlightenment, you'll chuckle quietly at the realization that you were 'here' all along!

In the meantime it still 'seems' you are far from being silent and still. Far from being able to view the changing scenes of life around you with complete equanimity and equipoise. Far from knowing the immense creative power that can come through the still being that you are. So until that awareness is fully restored, until you are fully present to your self, until you are no longer under the illusion of needing to go somewhere 'there' and you are fully 'here' again, here is a simple practice that may ease your way back to where you never left!

Just Notice

Sit somewhere quietly for a moment. Watch your thoughts. Notice there is you, and there are thoughts. Notice, as thoughts pass through your awareness, there are small gaps between each thought, like gaps between the carriages of a train. Now watch the gaps. As you do, notice how the gaps expand and your thoughts become slower. Notice within the gaps there is nothing. In that nothingness is stillness. There is silence. Notice the silence and allow it to expand. Notice there is no separation between you and the silence. Notice how 'still' you are, in the expanding silence.

Be in that silent and still state, without noticing anything! Then, when you return to noticing, take note of how you lost all awareness of time passing, all awareness of your form and the space around it, while you were fully 'here', and now, in the silent stillness of your being.

Question:
What is the difference between being and doing?

Reflection:
Nothing real ever changes - true or false?
If so, why? If not, why not?

Action:
Practise 'noticing', as in the final paragraph above,
for three minutes twice a day for the next week.

The 7 Masks of Zorrow!

It's often forgotten that one of the dragons that must be slain on the road to happiness is the cause of sorrow. It seems likely that few of us will clearly see what brings our spirit down, simply because it's too close to home. It is so close, so subtle and very often so subconscious! It's those moments when we are trying to be someone we are not, without realizing it. Those moments can last from a few minutes to a lifetime! They are not easy to spot because they are events that originate and happen entirely within our consciousness. It doesn't help to realize it's what we have been taught to do. Unless we have developed a 'fine' degree of self-awareness we won't be able to recognize when we are trying not to be our self!

The basic principle is: If you try to be anything or anyone other than your self, then some fear and sadness will always cause a loss of happiness as a result.

Unreal Image

A good analogy to describe the origins of such moments of sorrow is the mannequin party. Everyone turns up holding a mask on a stick in front of their face, which makes them almost (but not quite) impossible to recognize. You could say that they are both hiding and, at the same time, attempting to project an unreal image of themselves. Without being fully aware of it we do the same within our consciousness when we create what is known as a 'subtle self image'.

It's as if we hold the self-image, like a mask, in front of our consciousness and we attempt to 'wear' and be that image/mask. All our thoughts, feelings and behaviors are then 'shaped by' and 'flow from' that self-image.

There are of course many 'gross' or obvious self-images that we have all learned to create and hide ourselves behind. These include images based on what our bodies look like, what we do, the group that we 'believe' we belong to or align with (from a football team to a religion!), our family history, our nations etc. We create and use such images to define our sense of identity and depending on the situation and circumstances we will switch between these images, which is like switching masks, as we wander through the fancy dress party we call life! This is probably one reason why we have an identity crisis in the world in general,

"We start switching masks, as we wander through the fancy dress party we call life!"

and why many people in particular, will at some stage of their life spend time and energy searching for themselves, as they try to solve the 'who am I...really' conundrum! It takes a little while to realize I am/you are/we are all no one! But that's another seminar!

In the meantime, while we may realize the obvious i.e. that we are not what we do, not what we look like in the mirror and not where we were born, we will probably find it hard to see the more 'subtle masks' that we wear during the course of an average day. There are many. They are all sources of sorrow simply because we are trying to be someone we are not, which is naturally unnatural!

Here are seven of many masks, many subtle self images that we create and identify our self with. What you might call The 7 Masks of Zorrow! Which of the following masks do you recognize within your self most strongly?

The Sensible Mask

If you are a regular creator and wearer of this self-image you will tend to consider yourself to be the person who always does the right thing, the reasonable thing, the common sense thing. You tend to think, "I am the one to bring some grounded sense to you and your/this situation". You want to be seen by others as balanced, stable, sensibly correct and correctly sensible! You will be quickly on hand to give good advice and guidance the moment you sense something might be 'going south'! You will allow yourself the feeling of satisfaction once your advice has been dispensed, but you will become easily frustrated at the sight of others doing what you consider to be stupid and nonsensical. And then you'll worry that others won't actually follow your advice, which is why you can so easily and regularly lose your happiness.

The Mask of Shame

You wear this mask as soon as you think 'I have done something wrong', which is frequently. You will even watch and identify with others wrong doings and feel guilty on their behalf. Your most frequent thoughts include, "I messed up again...I always get this wrong... I am not able to do this without letting someone down". Seeing your self as guilty is easy if you had a childhood full of judgemental parents or scolding teachers and regular insinuations that, "You are wrong again!" The built in sadness that lives at the heart of guilt and shame will always be waiting to prick any bubble of genuine happiness.

The Subservient Mask

When you wear this mask you bow down to others in your mind. You hold others as greater than you. Thoughts emerge like, "I wish I could do that...I can never be that good...I am just lucky to know them", are all signs that your self-image is always of 'smallness' in comparison to others. As you suppress your self in this way you suppress your natural happiness, making any lasting contentment impossible.

The Superior Mask

You wear this mask when you think of your self as the one who doesn't just know, but 'knows everything' the most clearly and the most deeply. You think of yourself as the 'greater one', the one who has a solution to every problem. You will be an air of superiority and an attitude of 'I know better'. This is a self-image that guarantees you will see others as threats to your throne. There will be the fear that maybe you don't know best/deepest/clearest and that 'they' actually do. This will gnaw away at your happiness on the inside but you probably won't notice it...too much! And you certainly won't show it...too often!

The Seductive Mask

This is the mask of the needy, worn when you want others attention so that you can feel valued. You attempt to attract others energy to you. This is not referring to 'seductive' at a physical level. That gross self-image based on form has already been transcended. Seductive here means the elegant words, the flattering observations, the warmest compliments, all expressed in ways that are mentally and emotionally attractive

"The arrogance that sits in behind this mask is always swinging between fear and anger."

to 'the other'. You then create and carry a certain pride when others gravitate towards you as a result of what you believe to be your magnetic attractiveness. This becomes a dragon that needs to be fed regularly and when the food is threatened, as it will be every day, the anxiety will dispatch any happiness with clinical efficiency.

The Sensitive Mask

This is a popular mask worn when you see yourself as the one who cares most and best. You are always on the lookout for opportunities to 'be there' for others in their emotional and personal crisis. When you wear the sensitive mask you will think, "Only I can appreciate what you are going through...only I can help you to deal with your life challenges... only I can sense what's really going on here." The arrogance that sits in behind this mask is always swinging between fear and anger. Fear that you may miss something and lose your reputation as the 'oh so sensitive and caring one'. And anger that others might not allow you to get fully under their skin in order to fully sense and understand what they are going through so that you can be seen to care for and about them! And so your happiness will be fleeting and dependent on the one for whom you are being so sensitive.

The Mask of Sorrow

Well they are all masks that induce sorrow but the king of all the masks is the self-image based on sorrowfulness. It is worn most frequently when you decide to feel sorry for yourself. Even when you may be shouting at others, "I don't want your pity", you are probably pitying yourself because you have attracted the pity of others! On the one hand you use others pity to enhance your sorrowful self-image, and then you fervently reject it and make yourself feel isolated with the thought, "Am I the only one who feels sorry for me around here?".

All these subtle self-images, that we create and wear as masks on the inside, are of course the 'ego at work'. It is just a subtler level of the habit of creating and identifying with something we are not. That something is always an image, or a concept, or an idea, or just a belief.

Obviously none of these masks is ever the true self. They can never be the 'real' I. The true face behind the masks is the creator and wearer of the masks. It is the face that can never be seen. Being at peace and feeling authentic happiness is only possible when we have no mask. That's when we are aware of our self as the faceless face...so to speak!

But for most of us that can sound a bit...scary!
So up pops Scary Mask!

Questions:
Which of the seven masks do you think you tend to
create and wear most frequently?

Reflection:
How would you describe the precise nature of your
Sorrow when you hide behind this mask?

Action:
Watch for those sorrowful feelings this coming week and as soon as you
become aware of them take off your mask
and see what difference it makes

"Being at peace and feeling authentic happiness is only possible when we wear no mask."

Why it's Impossible
to Love YOUR Self

There is a statement that is often heard during personal development workshops. It's been written in countless books. It is one of the mantras of what became known as 'new age' thinking. It's the moment when someone says, "I need to learn to love my self".

In their determination to generate more 'self love' many have gone straight to 'mirror mirror on the wall' and started to repeat their new self-affirmation, "I love my self" at the image of their face. And then wondered why not much changes! Which is not surprising as the face that we see in the mirror is neither the 'I' nor the 'self'. It is the physical mask that we inhabit and wear.

Loving your face and therefore your body, believing both to be what 'I am', only strengthens your attachment to and identification with your body. And that's not love, it's attachment! It's likely to create and strengthen a combination of vanity and narcissism. That, in turn, only generates more anxiety, as both face and body are obviously in a permanent state of decay!

So 'loving my self' is not loving my body. But that's not to say our body does not require care. It is, after all, our personal limousine, so we do need to look after it!

Thousand Lines

Then there are those who write a thousand times the self instruction/affirmation, "I love my self". Somewhat reminiscent of the 'thousand lines' of punishment at school! Even as they repeat their self-loving affirmation they too will eventually wonder why nothing much changes. It takes time to realize that it takes more than one 'thought', regardless of how often it is repeated, to change how we 'feel' within and about our self. They probably don't notice that to concentrate hard, or repetitively, on any one thought, actually suppresses their feelings.

The repetition of one thought also becomes a little boring. So some start to expand the idea into, "I am learning to accept my self" or "I am becoming kind to my self" or "I am compassionate towards my self" or "I am learning to forgive my self". But without 'feeling' the authentic power of love, these thoughts too will only have a brief and limited benefit, and therefore a somewhat brief and limited lifespan. You can't 'think' your way to love.

Loving Others

The 'I love myself' philosophy and ideology is also underlined by the equally common belief that you cannot love others, or even just one other, until you are able to love your self. It sounds logical and seems to make sense. Then, when some find they don't want to love another or are unable to give love to others, they often then conclude that they are not yet loving enough of their self!

"You can't think your way to love."

Then they blame themselves for not loving themselves enough. They diminish themselves even more as they see themselves failing to live up to others and their own expectations. So it's off to another workshop or seminar to remind and re-affirm that they can still learn to 'love my self'!

This process can easily continue in a kind of repetitive cycle for some time, often years, until maybe one day we have our 'light bulb moment' and the penny drops on the realization that it's not possible to 'love my self'! It's a mission that is impossible to complete. It is a task, an aim, and a goal that is doomed to a predictable and inevitable failure! But why?

Which One Am I?

Love is a name for the pure awareness and radiant light of the conscious being that we are. But only when we are free of all attachment, which means free of all attempts to possess, hold on, own, acquire or desire anything or anyone. Why, because each of these habits generates fear. If you watch and get to know your own feelings you will see this clearly for your self!

Fear is love distorted by attachment. It's the same energy (of consciousness, which IS the self) but a different vibration, a different frequency, hence a very different 'feeling'. When you 'feel love' you are free of all urges to grasp, possess, acquire, desire, so the energy of your consciousness, which is you, radiates freely outwards into the world.

"To say, "'I love my self", only sustains an illusion that there is an 'I' and a 'self'."

Love is what I/you/we are whenever we give of our self, with the intention to benefit another, while wanting nothing in return. In such moments love is what the 'I' that says 'I am' is! It is your self! It is YOU!

However, for many of us, after a lifetime of 'habitually wanting', this is such a rare personal 'insperience' that we try to induce such feelings by watching 'others' apparently being loving. We then live vicariously through their relationships and interactions as they appear to have found love or are being love. This is why Hollywood has the world mesmerized by stories and dramas constructed out of 'romantic love'. We generally don't realize that it's not love we're watching but attachment. Hence the emotions of sadness, frustration and anxiety that make-up all the fictional 'dramas' that we allow our self to be sucked into.

One or Two ME's

To say, "I love my self ", only sustains an illusion that there is an 'I' and a 'self ', when, in truth, there is only the 'I' that says 'I am'. The 'I' is the 'self' and the self is love itself! Just as the eye cannot see itself and the finger cannot touch itself, so you cannot love your self. Love cannot love love! Neither the self nor love is an object. Love just 'is' because you just 'are'. But only when you are non-attached!

This level of 'self-realization' completely alters your understanding of what love is and where it is. It ceases to be something that you believe can be sought, found and known only through a special relationship, as depicted by Hollywood in particular and marketing in general, into something that can never be 'acquired'! It may be received, but you no longer need to acquire it when you realize it is what you are. This realization also dissolves that other common misbelief, that love is something that is 'required', and therefore sourced outside your self, revealing an awareness of 'the self' as a source of love in the world.

The Search is Over

Realizing love is what you are, frees you from the 'great search' for love. Then the question arises, "If love is what I am why don't I feel loving and know my self as love"? By 'living in' this question you will start to see and realize what's in the way of you being your self, of you being love itself. You will likely realize that ultimately love is never lost, just as 'you' can never be lost from your self! You simply sabotage the quality of the vibration of your consciousness, which is your self, by becoming attached to...anything or anyone!

Attachment is the primary symptom of the 'search for love'. Attachment always generates fear in it's many forms including of anxiety and worry, which are always signs that you are looking in the wrong place for love!

From Me to You

Perhaps the simplest answer to the question 'how do I know love is what I am' is as follows:

Only when you give what you HAVE within you, do you know what you ARE. Only when you give what you ARE do you know what you HAVE! Which is why, when you give that gift 'with love', you are the first to know and feel that love... 'on the way out'! When you say, "This is from me to you with love", you might as well say, "This is from me to you with the energy of me"!

Only when you 'give out' what you are, do you know that what you 'have within' is the same as what you are! And when you give, with love, that's when you realize your self as love. It's just that in such moments you are not thinking 'I am love'! But notice how the last thought that would ever enter your mind in such a moment is 'I need to learn to love my self'. Why would you, how could you, when you know your self as love itself?

From that moment on, whenever you read or hear someone saying that line, "I need to learn to love my self", you recognize it's just code for, "I need to find love/get love/be loved because I have not yet realized I am love!". Then you can ask them. "Which one are you? Are you the 'I' or the 'self'? Or are you the 'me', the one who says, "Me, my self and I?" Now who needs to love who... in here?"

Extracted and adapted from the book:
The 7 Myths About LOVE...Actually!
Unravelling the Mysteries of Love.

Are YOU a Victim, a Student or a Master?

Life means change and change signifies the flowing and flowering nature of life. Like a river, life is always on the move. Unfortunately we tend to learn that we have to 'damn the river' as we try to stop the flow and 'hold on' to a) the way things are and b) what we think we have acquired from the river itself! This is known as the 'Damn It!' philosophy of change management! This philosophy is guaranteed to create a stressful journey as we frequently whisper 'damn it' to ourselves! A few however, will learn to practice the 'Judo' philosophy of change management, continuously letting go of the old so that they can welcome and 'embrace the new', thereby creating ways to flow with, and not against, the river.

Do YOU fear change? Are you practising the Damn It! philosophy? Do you find yourself resisting people and situations? Any form of resistance anywhere, anytime, means you fear change. It means you 'believe' you are about to lose something, as any kind of fear is always the sign of 'imagined' future loss. The seven most common things that people fear losing when their resistance starts to show up are the 7 Ps - position, power, pay, possessions, people, prestige, privileges.

In the past two decades the 'change management industry', established and sustained by an army of highly paid consultants and trainers, have preached their gospels on how to meet, measure, manage and be a master of change in the world. One of their mantras is: *the only thing in this world that doesn't change is change itself.* But it looks like they may have missed the main trick! For there is something else that never changes and that is 'the one' that observes change happening. The one who watches, witnesses and waits on change is none other than ones 'self'. It is the one and only thing that never comes and goes! But then again, 'it's' not a 'thing'! The 'I' that says 'I am' is not a thing!

The idea of 'change management' implies that change can be controlled. But the real 'master of change' knows that they can neither control any change in the world 'out there' and nor do they need to. And they definitely do not want to! But they are aware that they can 'influence' the flow of change.

"Masters of change are fully aware but undisturbed by anything that happens around them."

The **master** of change has realized that change at all levels, from the material to the mental, from events to circumstances, is like background music in a movie, it simply plays through, behind and around every scene. The symphony of life is called change. And the symphony is always playing out exactly as it should.

The **master** knows that the less you want to 'control' how the river of life is destined to flow the more you will be an 'influence' on how and where the river flows. The enlightened soul focuses not on controlling the process of change, but on the consciousness that perceives the nature of change. They know that it is our state of consciousness that is the most powerful influence on the direction of the change it will focus on.

Many of us perpetually see ourselves as **victims of change**, always blaming and complaining about how life is getting in the way of our happiness. Some are **students of change**, attempting to work out why life throws up certain people, events and circumstances in their path the way it does. They are always looking for better techniques and methods to not be affected and stressed by the unexpected and unwanted. A few are **masters of change**, fully aware and yet undisturbed by anything that happens around them.

The **victim** of change experiences life as continuous source of stress. For the **student** of change life is both a struggle and a teacher, depending on what's going on exactly, and their state of mind at the time. For the **master** of change life is a dance. The consultants and the trainers need victims and students of change, *"Many of us perpetually see ourselves as victims of change, always blaming and complaining about how life is getting in the way."* otherwise they would be out of a job! The last thing they want in their strategy meetings or their classrooms is a master of change, as they would likely have to become the student!

So what are you, how do you consider your self, as a victim, a student or a master? Here are some of the other signs and symptoms of each and an opportunity to see where your MINDSET sits along the 'change spectrum'.

Perception of Change

The **victim** of change is always singing the song of, "Why is this happening to me?", as they attribute their loss of peace and happiness to someone or something 'out there'. The **student** of change endeavors to view any changes in the world 'out there' that are about to have an impact on the way they live and work, not as events that might force them to lose something, but as opportunities to gain something.

They are practitioners of 'the shift' from the 'Damn It' philosophy of change management, which states that you must hang on to everything in your life and keep things the way they are, to the 'Judo' philosophy of change management. This approach is based on the understanding that all change is simply different forms of energy coming towards you and the wise thing to do is embrace it, and then make it's direction and momentum work for you.

"The change student is continuously struggling to overcome feelings of separation, isolation and aloneness when they meet the challenges of a changing world."

The **student's** aim is therefore to enact a shift in their perception of change from 'possible loss' to 'probable gain'. The change **master** on the other hand has already realized they have nothing to lose for they know that 'in reality' they possess nothing. They never feel 'threatened' by any event in the continuously changing world 'out there'. Free of the belief in loss, free of the desire to gain, they are free to meet life as it happens wholeheartedly, without prejudice, preference or expectation.

Capacity to Cope

In any enclosed 'change process', as happens within organizations, the **victim** of change can only handle so much. They quickly reach their limit and shout, "Enough is enough, I can't take any more". Or they start to fight with those who seem to be initiating the changes. The change **student**, on the other hand, either a) seeks to understand why things around here need to change or b) endeavors to see their changing situation as an opportunity to increase their capacity to cope and learn.

The change **master** has reached a point where they no longer have to cope with anything. They have realized the very nature of life outside the self is 'change' but that the true nature of the self is stillness. They know that around stillness change must inevitably flow, like water around a rock. The change master is like a rock. Their life is touched by the changing world, but never shaken, never disturbed. They allow change to flow around and through their life, but they are no longer shaped by it. If ever they are, they use it to make themselves more 'rounded'.

Ready, Willing and Able

The change **victim** is always complaining about their stress. Any signs of stress means they are either not *ready* for the world to change, not *willing* to face change or they are not *able* to deal effectively with whatever changes are happening.

The change **student** may have recognized that the pace of change in the world is only going to continue accelerating. They are therefore continuously 'working' on preparing themselves in order to be more *ready*, more *willing* and more *able* to deal with whatever comes when it comes. Their learning revolves around a conscious effort to shift from 'reacting' to 'responding', thereby restoring self-control in the face of 'the uncontrollable'.

To the change **master** there are no surprises! They are always able to respond appropriately. They don't have to 'get' *ready*, for they are always ready. They don't have to become *willing* to face whatever happens, as they have no intention of avoiding anything or anyone. And they don't have to develop their *ability* to deal with change as their ability has already been developed, usually through the process of graduating from victim, to student to master.

Alone or Lonely

With the tendency to take things personally, the **victim** of change frequently feels abandoned and alone. The change **student** may struggle to overcome feelings of separation and isolation, but they will likely learn to hold out their hand and assist others to cope with the changes knowing, that as they help others, they help themselves. The change **master**, on the other hand, never feels isolated in a changing world for they know that everything is unbreakably interconnected at a more invisible level. They are always available to support others through the challenges that change must bring to those who have not yet graduated from the school of mastery!

They know and are constantly aware that we are all 'in this' (game of life) together. The change **master** never feels lonely for they know and accept separation as a natural condition of the material world. They know that at the level of the material world they are always alone! Connected yet separated, alone but never lonely, the change masters universe 'seems' to be filled with such paradoxes and apparent contradictions. But to the change master themselves there are no contradictions, no paradoxes, for all is 'one' in the primary reality of their own consciousness.

Mastering change is not about using pre-designed or learned techniques, strategies or tools. Becoming a **master** of change is the realization of a completely new perception of the world and of ones role in the world. From their still and silent center the change **master** sees that the world around them is in a constant state of flux, it is simply the energies of life rising and falling, ebbing and flowing, waxing and waning. It is nature's way!

From this awareness the master acts, which means 'creates their response', from inside out, informed and shaped by a wisdom that is found in the unchanging stillness of their being, and not from the exhortations, demands, desires or the pleas of others.

The change **victim** is continuously crying out, "Why is this happening TO me?" The change **student** says to themselves, "Why is this happening FOR me?" The change **master** is quietly aware that, "All change is happening THROUGH me!" They have realized that the primary reality in which change takes place is not out there in the big wide world of time and space, but 'in here' in the big wide inner space of their own consciousness.

They have fully realized that 'it's not what happens around me that makes me feel this way, it's what I do with what happens around me that makes me feel this way'!

Question:
Where on the spectrum – victim, student, master - would you currently position your self during your average day?

Reflection:
When things happen in some parts of the world they say, "Don't just sit there, do something!" But in other parts of the world they say, "Don't just do something, sit there!" Why the different responses and what is the difference between the two?

Action:
Awareness exercise - take five minutes at the end of each day this week, review the day, and decide in which mode you were in (victim/student/master) at various points during the day.

Dealing with the Loss of a Loved One

In response to a question - **How can we help someone who is in the process of losing a loved one?**

One of the greatest challenges in life that we all may face one day is the loss of a loved one. Our response is 'likely' to range across a spectrum from mild but significant sadness to the feeling of utter devastation and desolation – who knows, until it actually happens.

Preparing our self for such an eventuality is not to invoke it, nor is it to indulge in some morbid mental fantasy. It is a preparation that can help us to support others as they deal with the loss of a loved one either before or during their grief. So the first step, if we are to hold out a consoling and supporting hand for others, is to sense how we ourselves might deal with such a loss in our own life.

Reality Check

The form that we occupy is perishable and each one of us has our destined moment of departure from our mortal coil. That's a basic reality in all our lives. Prior to such an event we could remind our self that there is nothing more inevitable in life than death. Acceptance of the inevitability of death is not to invite it, nor is it to give up on living, but simply coming to terms with the truth of a universal reality. Some people even use this truth to ensure that they live fully and waste no 'living time'. It's almost impossible to control our departure date. Mentally struggling against its future inevitability only begets a futility that easily drains any happiness we have in the here and now. Not to mention the waste of energy!

Common Illusion

When we say that we have lost, or are about to lose, a loved one, we could also remind our self that our loss is a delusion, that the 'losing' of someone is impossible, as they weren't ours to 'possess' in the first place. Any sadness/sorrow is always the result of a belief that something has been lost, which in turn is based on the belief that something has been possessed. But can we possess another human being? Obviously not! We even remind ourselves and others that we cannot possess anything when we say, "Well you can't take it with you when you go!"

"Any 'suffering' is a signal that we have temporarily disconnected from our true nature, which is peaceful, powerful and loving."

This is why any sadness/sorrow is based on the illusion that you 'had them' (possessed them) while they were here! That's not to say one should not be sad, or that it's bad to be sad. We are simply seeking to understand exactly why we make our self so sorrowful at the passing of someone close.

If we inquire further we may find our suffering is due to our confusing love with attachment ... again! Although we may know the theory of 'love is letting go', even when we know that all fear prior to loss, and all sadness after the moment of loss, is the result of our attachment (which we mistake for love), it's still hard not to suffer when the moment comes. So deeply has this habit 'to attach' seeped into our consciousness we even justify our tears by affirming another commonly held belief/illusion that says 'it's only natural to grieve', which is code for 'it's human nature and therefore natural to suffer'.

But is it? If we surrender to this one belief we may live our entire life unhappily and not realize we could have done something about it!

I suspect many do!

Our tears will continue to flow until we realize and remember that deeper truth, which reminds us that any 'suffering' is a signal that we have temporarily disconnected from our true nature, which is peaceful, powerful and loving. The strength offered by our true nature is only accessible when we have 'seen through' the delusion that attachment is a sign of love, the delusion that our tears signify our caring, the delusion that our emotional suffering is natural. These are not easy delusions to dispel in a world that affirms and celebrates them almost every day.

Don't Cry For Me!

In the midst of our sorrow following the departure of our 'loved one' (or should that now read our 'attached one'!) we could ask, as many do, would 'they' want us to suffer after they are gone? Would they thank us for our tears and our self-sustaining unhappiness? Highly unlikely! In fact they would probably say the opposite, as indeed some do before they go. They would more likely want us to get on with our life, be happy and be at peace. Would we not want those whom we leave behind to do the same? Or would we take pleasure in knowing that they are devastated following our exit from the stage of life?

Here They Come!

Then there is the spiritual answer to the death or the 'departure' of another, which reminds us that they don't actually die. They simply move out of their current physical form and are reborn in a new form. There is obviously no scientific evidence for this ancient belief about what happens when we die. But there is plenty of anecdotal evidence of 'rebirth' from young children carrying very clear memories of a previous life and from those who have undergone some form of regressive hypnosis. If we can 'intuit' any truth in the idea that the soul (the self) simply leaves the body at the moment we call death, then instead of being tearful we might 'send them off' with our good wishes and bountiful blessings for the next chapter on their grand adventure. Much like we might wish 'happy holidays' to friends on their way to their annual vacation.

This idea of the soul's journey is captured in the words of Victor Hugo from Toilers of the Sea in which he uses the metaphor of the ship sailing over the horizon:

A ship sails and I stand alone, watching till she fades on the horizon, and someone at my side says, "She is gone". Gone where? Gone from my side, that is all; she is in me just as large as when I saw her. The diminished size, and total loss of sight is in me, not in her, and just at the moment when someone at my sides says, "She is gone", there are others who are watching her coming, and other voices take up the glad shout. "There she comes!" And that is dying.

"Ultimately our fear of death is not a fear of the unknown but a fear of losing, of being separated from, what we already know!"

Perhaps this is why, in some cultures, they don't mourn death but celebrate it. They have a party to celebrate the life of a good friend and to send them on their way on a wave of love, good wishes and merriment. Yes please!

Dying Alive
Ultimately our fear of death is not a fear of the unknown but a fear of losing, of being separated from, what we know and what we 'believe' we have. This is why, for many, the idea of death itself is not a major issue; it is the manner of its accomplishment! If there is fear then it is often a fear of the amount of physical pain that may have to be endured as we slip through the 'exit door' at the end of the 'corridor of life'. But while the exact moment of our departure is

never known in advance it seems we can influence our own moment of dying, exit the physical body painlessly at the end of 'this chapter' and go in peace. This possibility is encapsulated by the saying, "If you die before you die then when you die you don't die". Otherwise known as 'dying alive', it simply means there can be a conscious choice to acknowledge and let go of everything to which we are attached.

Death, in this strand of spiritual wisdom, is painful only when we cling to our attachments while at the same time being wrenched away from them. Toys and children remind us of this grasping at the objects of life and the tears that easily flow when life asks for the toys to be returned. If we can learn to let go, before we are forced to release, we may be able to re-vision the 'end of the line' as a gliding return to home – a gradual, inevitable, flawless movement, an easy and natural farewell, the soul's ascent to its resting place, regardless of whatever is happening both within our body or around our body at that time.

If we can truly grasp this for our self then perhaps we can help others over the threshold by letting them go and then letting them know that we have let them go, while still 'being there' lovingly and caringly for them and with them, as they make their way out.

Final Moments

It's not easy, this dying business! But there seems to be ways to make it easier for our self, and then for others, when someone close is about to move on. In the process of exploring and understanding the true nature of our 'final moments' we also come to appreciate 'this life' for what it simply is; an amazing opportunity to live fully and joyfully that will not last forever. Besides, if someone offered us the chance to live for five hundred years would we take it?

In the process of helping someone who is in the process of losing someone close, perhaps it's not about saying any of the above but just sharing with them the quiet strength we ourselves may gain from contemplating the above. And if their curiosity is aroused perhaps that's the signal to explore more explicitly some of these possibly deeper truths about 'the inevitable'.

The 'end time' for each and every person is unique and unpredictable, requiring a moment-by-moment sensitivity and a sense of appropriateness that cannot be pre-scribed. This probably also applies for the one closest to the one who is leaving!

In being close to someone who is about to take their leave we are faced with, and some would say privileged to look in, a powerful mirror in which we get to see exactly where we stand in our relationship with death. In looking in the mirror of another's death we get glimpses of how much we value living our self, to what extent we are prepared to leave 'the party' and to what extent we are giving of our own life while no longer grasping at life.

Question:
Why do we fear death...really?

Reflection:
What is the meaning of 'dying alive' and why is it a
preparation for leaving your 'mortal coil'?

Action:
If you knew you only had six months to live
what would you do differently?

Do YOU Have a Hierarchy of Needs?

When asked, "Do you have needs?" most people answer almost immediately in the affirmative, "Yes of course I do!"

But are YOU sure?

The gospel according to Maslow is known as The Hierarchy of Needs. And 'gospel' it seems to be, in corners of the world far and wide! That we have specific needs, on a rising scale, seems to be a widely accepted set of truths, often quoted in seminars, books and conversations, which explore our place, purpose and predicament here on planet Earth! Seldom is the validity of those truths, probably better described as 'Maslow's Beliefs', seen to be challenged. So lets!

The idea of 'needs', and the opinion that we have some if not many, seems to have become a cornerstone of many schools of psychology, psychotherapy and numerous other therapies. Spirituality however would probably beg to differ. Some would say that from a 'spiritual point of view' we ultimately have no needs. Our body has needs but we/I/you don't! That's because, from a spiritual point of view, we are spirit and not the form that we occupy.

From the psychological/therapeutic viewpoint we are psycho-physical entities, which essentially means 'body' and 'self' are perceived to be one and the same. Hence the idea in Maslow's Hierarchy, that our primary needs are essentially based on being a physical entity with a physical identity. The spiritual understanding however, separates consciousness from form, soul from body. But how might that perspective cast a new meaning over Maslow's Hierarchy and alter our mindset regarding our 'needs'?

What is the Hierarchy?

First, a quick reminder of Maslow's hierarchy. According to Maslow our primary need is **Biological/Physical** i.e. the need for air, food, water, shelter and warmth. Then there is the need for **Security**, protection and order. Once satisfied we graduate to a need for a sense of **Belonging** so that love can be acquired and felt. Then it's the need for self **Esteem** based on things like achievement, status and reputation. And finally our highest, or should that be deepest, need is for **Self-actualization,** which is translated by various people in various ways including personal growth, reaching one's full potential and a sense of fulfillment.

"The realization of self as spirit not body, can ultimately free us from the fear (insecurity) of not getting our physical needs met, because they are not MY needs."

But are they really needs? Is it true that we cannot live full and happy lives until these needs, according to Maslow, are met? How does the idea that we are fundamentally a spiritual being, occupying and animating a physical form, change our interpretation of Maslow's Hierarchy?

The Basic BIOLOGOCAL/PHYSICAL Needs

Even at the most basic physical level the 'spiritual perspective' might cast a little doubt over the veracity of Maslow's ideas. From the spiritual perspective (i.e. I am spirit), when we acquire food/shelter/clothing etc. we are not doing so for 'me' but for our body i.e. the body that I occupy! Our first responsibility is for our body. Our body has needs. It needs us to take care of it.

When we make this distinction between what is sometimes called the 'authentic self' and 'my body', we gradually cease to identify with our body. This 'identity shift' alone can start to reduce our levels of insecurity. This is only possible when the self realizes its self as a spiritual entity that does not 'need' air, food or shelter etc.! If there is a need it sounds more like, "I need to take care of my body. My body needs food, shelter and air etc.". This is quite different to, "I need to take care of me", which is what we are thinking when our sense of identity is based just on our body. *Giving* care to our body is quite different from *desiring* something for me!

Giving and caring springs from love whereas desiring always has its roots in fear and insecurity. This means the 'spiritual perspective' i.e. the realization of self as spirit not body, can begin to free us from the fear (insecurity) of not meeting the physical needs of my body, because they are not MY needs. It can also begin to liberate us from the 'survivalist mindset', (fear) allowing us to operate from a higher intention, which is a more 'caring for the other' mindset. (love)

The Need for SECURITY

One of the most common observations that arises from the awareness of self as an invisible, spiritual entity, animating and expressing through a material form, is 'permanence of being'. It takes a few moments (with a little practice) to notice that everything changes. All 'things' come and go. Material 'things', including all forms 'out there', come and go. Mental 'things' including all thoughts and feelings 'in here', come to pass... literally! And they do! But the one and only thing that never passes or goes anywhere is the pure awareness that is 'self'. If this is fully 'realized', as it seems to have been by many in their search for enlightenment, then security and survival cease to be relevant or valid issues to be concerned about. While bodies cease to be, the spirit that we/I/you are, doesn't!

When the self is 'fully realized' as the pure and permanent awareness that never passes, there is no need for security, as the 'spiritual truth' about the permanence of the self, when realized, can never be threatened. The belief that we need to be secure arises from the belief that we are nothing more than the ever changing, temporary material forms that we occupy. Physical forms can be threatened and destroyed by nothing more than natural decay! But we believe we are transient when we believe we are just a form. That's why the 'belief' in ones own transience is like a cancer in the soul. Its primary symptom is a free-floating anxiety in the background of all our days!

Besides, if we 'believe' we have a 'need' for security we find ourselves continuously fearing and fending off insecurity, which results in... perpetual insecurity!

The Need for BELONGING and LOVE

A need for belonging is often confused with the search for a sense of identity. We learn to identify with 'ideas' like family, club, profession, nation, religion and race etc. From each of these identities we can 'seem' to derive a 'feeling' of belonging. We don't notice however, that in each case we are attempting to externalise our sense of self. We are trying to find our self outside of our self. From a spiritual point of view this is a form of insanity! At the very least it is extremely non-spiritual! It is also what gives rise to the ego otherwise known as the 'false self' or misidentification. This then leads to feelings of fragmentation, isolation and unhappiness simply because each of these 'externalised identities' are limited, they change, and they can therefore be threatened.

Once again the news from those who seemed to have transcended this search for belonging (finding an externalised identity) tells us that we already belong. They report on a sense of connection that is invisible, subtle and both transcendent and transformative. They remind us that we are 'no thing'; that we are pure light, pure awareness i.e. a conscious being that no longer needs nor desires to identify with any 'thing'!

This realisation, that we have no identity at all, is not a loss of self, nor a vacuum that we fall into, but the restoration of an awareness of just 'being me', the unbounded awareness just prior to the first thought 'I am'. By all accounts this is the ultimate liberation, the ultimate freedom, while still in and acting through ones material form. From this state of awareness, 'they say', there arises a deep sense of interconnectedness, a natural peace and the simple innocent joy of living. However it is a 'state of being' (awareness) that we can only ever 'know' for sure by going there and being there! Not a journey that fits easily into a busy schedule!

"If we 'believe' we have a need for security we find ourselves continuously fearing and fending off insecurity, which results in perpetual insecurity!"

And as for love, when we realise love is what we are, then the need (which is really a desire) to find it, acquire it and keep it, falls away. It is replaced by the giving of love in whatever way is appropriate to the situation/scene/circumstances etc. Only then is true love known. If there is 'a natural need' in relation to love it is to give it!

The Need for ESTEEM

When esteem is 'believed' to be dependent on and defined by achievement, status and reputation, we can see how this 'apparent need' drives much of human activity in the world today. Even at the cost of the other so-called needs. Esteem essentially means *estimation,* which means *valuation,* which means *worth.* Increasingly we are aware of the pitfalls of basing our sense of worth on achievement, which is always momentary; on status, which can be lost at any moment; and on our reputation, which can be destroyed by a few keystrokes! When our self worth, and therefore esteem, is based on such transient and delicate external aspects of life, it actually generates greater feelings of insecurity and the frequent loss of perceived worthiness.

Once again the spiritual point of view reveals an awareness of real worth as something that is only found deep within the self... itself! It is an awareness of our value that arises only from the act of giving of our self without seeking any return. It is the realisation of self as a source of love, as a source of life energy that is innately creative and with the capacity to empower others. Arising in parallel to this inner source of 'worth' is the awareness of the impossibility of loss, which is the foundation for the ultimate sense of security. To the being that has restored and 'lives from' their true self-awareness nothing 'real' can ever be lost forever.

The Need for SELF-ACTUALIZATION

From a spiritual point of view the idea of self-actualisation means self-realisation. In order to crystalize ones true potential one first has to realise who/what one is. Someone who knows they are a spiritual being (animator of form but not form itself) has no need to grow or fulfil anything. They are intuitively aware that they are already all they can ever be i.e. nothing need be developed, nothing real can be added to our authentic self. Fulfilment is already a reality i.e. they are aware they already endowed with the capacity to be loving, peaceful and creative.

However, they are also likely to be aware that the capacity to love (to connect openly and fully with others and the world) and be creative has been blocked and distorted by the conditioned beliefs of the world. Beliefs such as: 'you are only what you see in the mirror' or 'it's quite natural to be angry and unhappy' or 'success must be measured by material worth' or 'you need to satisfy certain needs before you can be fulfilled'! These kinds of beliefs all serve to suppress the awareness of the unlimited and infinitely joyous underlying nature that lies in the heart of every human being. Not the physical heart but the heart of consciousness.

From Belief to Truth

In the meantime it's not bad or wrong to believe that we have these needs. It's just not 'ultimately' true... from a spiritual point of view! The key word here is 'ultimately'. As we journey from belief to truth, as we make our way back to our natural state of being, beyond all neediness, we won't do too much harm in trying to satisfy any of those 'apparent' needs. It's just that we tend to turn needs into desires without noticing, and then they become 'greeds' and dependencies. That's when the train leaves the rails. But that's another seminar!

In conclusion, it seems from a spiritual point of view Maslow's hierarchy may be the wrong way round! When we attend to and achieve self-actualization first, which in essence means self-realization, everything else falls into place. When you know who you are as a spiritual being you cease to base your self-esteem/worth on anything outside of your self. It is innate and can never be lost. So 'insecurity' disappears and a natural sense of security takes its place.

When you know your self as spirit you cease to seek a sense of who you are 'out there', you cease to seek an identity in the world. You no longer feel the need to belong, which really means feel a part of something external, which really means you are looking for something to complete you, because you are already and always whole in your self. And you 'know' it!

And when you know your self as spirit, as the conscious and complete being that animates the form that occupy, you fully 'recognise' your responsibility to take care of your body's needs. But that now happens naturally. As a consequence of an accurate relationship with your body based on 'giving care' to the body as opposed to 'taking pleasure' from the body, your energy is free of dependency and fear. You are no longer busy with your own sensual pleasures and the accompanying anxieties, and more available to give to others, care for others, which makes you of value to others. This is then reciprocated at other levels including the physical level. As the old saying goes, what you give out you get back. And so it becomes easier to take care of your body's needs.

Beyond ALL Neediness

But what of those other less physical needs that we learn to believe we need to satisfy. What of the need for purpose, for goals, for meaning in life? Well, even those, more esoteric needs, may not be genuine needs in the end. You could say we *need* a purpose in life until we *don't need* a purpose. That freedom happens when we realise life has no purpose other than to live! You could say that we *need* goals until we *don't need* goals. That happens when we realise that a goal is just another desire and all desire is ultimately unnecessary when we are re-aligned with the natural flow of life. We *need* meaning until we *don't need* meaning. We *need* to be loved until we *don't need* to be loved, which means we have realised that love is what we are. We *need* a temporary identity/s until we rediscover and realise our true underlying awareness of who we really are, which is no body and no thing!

Perhaps it sounds a bit scary, but as so many of those ancient sages and saints have reminded us, these are final doorways to the ultimate liberation, the ultimate freedom from... all neediness! Through those doorways, 'they say', our bliss, our greatest happiness, awaits us. Then you don't need it! You are it!

Question:
Which one of the above needs do you tend to spend
the most time and energy pursuing?
Reflection:
If, in truth, you are not who you 'believe' you are, what are all the different
identities that you have learned to create for your self
that are just 'misbeliefs' about your self?
Action:
Try a day (or a week) this week of 'neediness awareness' i.e. consciously
notice all the situations and relationships in which you believe you
have to acquire something tangible or intangible from others
to meet your 'apparent' needs.

What is Success for YOU?

Most of us learn that success equals some form of achievement in the world. For many it's not the achievement but the recognition and the applause that they crave. For others it's not the arrival but the journey that generates the satisfaction of success. They value the process more than the prize. For some the pursuit of success will be avoided at all costs, sometimes for fear of failure, and sometimes for the fear of... success! And, for a few, just living simply and sincerely each day will be deemed to be successful enough!

"We learn to speak the common language of 'not enoughness' or 'scarcity'."

At some stage, in all our lives, there's a good chance we will each stop and consider the question, "What does success mean to me?" even if it's only for a few fleeting minutes! However, if we don't contemplate this question deeply then it's likely we will blindly follow other's ideas, beliefs and measures of success, usually learned in childhood, craved in youth and then pursued into our adult years.

We may not notice the connection between our dissatisfactions and the absence of a consciously defined and chosen idea of a what 'successful life' looks like and feels like. It is the clarity of an inner vision of success and wisdom about success that gives focus to our energies. It also adds to the sense that we are creating a meaningful life.

So what price success? That's the note that many of the modern day 'success gurus' begin and end on. It means how much are you prepared to sacrifice to achieve the success you want. How hard are you prepared to work? What are you willing to do to get there? Interesting questions, but they do make it all sound like hard work!

How do YOU define success? Is it simply the completion of the next task, another job well done, a promise kept, an exam passed, a medal won, a mountain climbed, a target hit, a happy family raised or the leaving of a legacy that ensures you will be remembered long after you have gone? Whatever you 'believe' success to be it will have a profound influence on your life. If you were to follow the predominant mindset in the world today then success would likely be measured by acquisition. The 'more' you have the more successful you will be seen to be.

More and Higher

When we inherit and absorb the prevalent 'beliefs' that the world is a place of scarcity, that the purpose of life is survival, that we must accumulate stuff to prosper, and that the more you get the happier you will feel, then success equals 'more'. More can be almost any quantity - objects, money, properties, trophies, celebrity, fame, fans, likes! And in the context of 'position', success simply means higher.

When we are taught to believe there is not enough to go around the media delights in keeping us abreast of upcoming shortages. If there aren't any obvious ones they will likely invent them for us! So we learn to speak the common language of `not enoughness' or 'scarcity'. We then struggle and strive for what we consider is our rightful share of the 'great pie', before someone else gets it, and 'more' is not only good, but applauded when attained. Hence, for many, if not most, 'more' simply equals success.

So what does it mean to you to be successful? At what level, in what context and by whose standards will you measure your success?

It's Immaterial!

If you were to give yourself some time to live in this question you would likely arrive at the fairly obvious insight that, at the deepest level, success in life is not a material thing, it is not something that can be possessed, or won, or even attracted! It is a state of being. Some call it contentment, or happiness, or even peace. Why, after all, does anyone want 'more' of anything? Because they believe these inner states will result. These feelings are, for some, the deepest and most meaningful 'symptoms of success', but only when these states of being are internally stable and consistent and therefore not dependent on anything outside ourselves. In other words not dependent of 'more' of anything!

"Is it not unnatural to be closed and narrow at any time and in any area of life?"

In the meantime success for most of us tends to be 'context specific'. As we consider 'context' we start to see why the kind of success we have been encouraged to pursue has many 'levels' and more than a few flaws.

The Context of SPORTING Success - in this context it's obviously about competition and winning. It's about being number one and being recognized and glorified by others as the one/s who took the prize. How often are we reminded that no one remembers the runner up? But few seem to ask why would I want to be remembered? Should the desire to be 'not forgotten' have a 'danger sign' hung around it that says 'ego at work'?

Notice how much physical and emotional suffering is required to reach the sporting peaks. Seldom do we see relaxed and contented sports people as they take their struggling and striving very seriously. They will say it's worth the pain. Others would say life was not meant to be a painful, tense and injurious affair, inflicted upon our self by our self!

Was all sport not originally based on games in which the 'joy of play', for the sake of playing, was given free reign? A time when faces smiled consistently and frustration, tension and anger were impossible.

The Context of BUSINESS Success - seems to range from building a large business to becoming highly profitable to being recognized for service excellence. Sometimes all three parameters are pursued, but unless they are prioritized there is the danger none will be achieved, leaving many stressed people in its wake. And if profit is prioritized over service it's fairly obvious that the energy behind the enterprise will become fear based and therefore quite an unhappy endeavor. Which may explain why many business people know stress intimately. It's a serious business... business! And, when the 'purpose of service' is lost and the profit motive kicks in, that's usually when need turns into greed and the ripple effect touches many far and wide. Hence the global financial turmoil that we see today.

> **"It's a serious business... business; which may explain why so many business people know stress so intimately".**

The Context of ACADEMIC Success - intellectual prowess tends to be the way this kind of success is measured and achieved, coupled with rather a good memory, naturally! It is often dependent on acquiring peer approval and driven by the desire to join a select club. It can easily result in an, 'I know the most and the best' attitude and a closed and narrow mindset that tends to characterize the so-called 'specialist' and the 'academic expert'. Is it not unnatural and therefore uncomfortable to be closed and narrow at any time and in any area of life? Unless you are a water pipe!

The Context of SCIENTIFIC Success - new theories, new dimensions of old theories, inventions of new technologies, the creation of new procedures, making fresh discoveries, all carry the 'success kite mark' in the scientific arena. Yet it tends to be all very material and 'out there', which tends to deny the other dimension we call spirit and the 'in here'. Scientific achievement certainly dominates our world today, but at what price we now ask, as we live increasingly isolated and technologically dependent lives, while sucking dry the natural wealth of the planet!

The Context of POLITICAL Success - tends to be measured by the acquisition of position and power, though much 'lip service' is given to the notion of public service. And while the intentions towards the upliftment of society are authentic and worthy we now know success in this arena is fragile, can be corrupted easily, and darker motives can often be found behind the desire to serve others. As more people rebel against the dictatorial political forces that have traditionally controlled our destiny, as more people demand a greater say in their fate, we now see the moral and ethical chaos that is generated as we/they realize and exercise new freedoms.

The Context of RELIGIOUS Success - once upon a time the pastoral care of a community provided the primary measure of a religions success. But religion has also become blurred and burdened by it's own structures and systems. Internal politics and power games, not to mention the fanatical adherence to belief and behavior systems that were invented hundreds of years ago in another age and in a completely different context, ensure the meaning of success in a religious context is increasingly blurred.

The Context of SPIRITUAL Success - is a state of being, sometimes referred to as enlightenment. But is it achieved or restored, or both? Perhaps its one fundamental difference from the other 'levels of success' is you wouldn't know someone has arrived at such an intangible and internal success unless you were in their presence for some time. Even then their simplicity and humility would probably deflect attention away from themselves. Can this form of incognito success still be classified as ...success?

That's not to say that success in any of the above arenas is not worth pursuing. As you form your mindset around success there is value in considering how success is viewed, defined and achieved in each context.

Inner Success

The whole idea of success takes on new meaning when we explore it in the context of our inner life. In this context personal success is the mastery of one's own ability to stay calm and focused, non-reactive and proactive, especially in challenging situations. When you start to build your inner capacities and attributes of self mastery, then all the other levels of success previously highlighted become easier to achieve, and yet, paradoxically, less relevant and/or much less meaningful.

Here are a few of the characteristics of self-mastery that signal your success at a deeper level than the material.

Inner success looks and feels more like the capabilities:

- to act with total honesty and integrity thus generating a clear conscience without which the authentic happiness that we call 'contentment' is impossible
- to remain peaceful and stable when all around you are in crisis or chaos
- to value what you are more than what you have
- to be able to see past the weaknesses/mistakes of others and focus on their inherent goodness/strengths
- to be able to let go of the past and thereby not allowing it to cloud your judgment in the present
- to give without the desire for anything in return

Notice how intangible these measures are. No one else can measure the efficacy of each or your success in implementing them, except your self. Notice how we seldom ask ourselves why we cannot achieve and maintain these inner states of being and the kind of enlightened behaviors that we would probably all desire all the time. Unless we 'can do and be' all of these it is unlikely we will achieve the deepest measure of success which is to be content within our self and able 'to give' our best to others without condition.

"The deepest success is perceived to be the ability to be the complete master of your consciousness while interacting with others."

As long as we desire to change the world, and that includes others, it means we are still trying to 'police the universe'. The enlightened soul however, has realized that is not 'my job'. They know that the light and power that emanates from a stable state of being, a contented state of being, from a giving intention, is one of the most influential gifts to others and to the world.

Success is Personal

As you reflect and contemplate on what success is going to look like and feel like for you, perhaps it's useful to include three key considerations.

1   Any success that is dependent on public recognition and acclaim will inevitably lead to insecurity and eventual depression, as does all forms of dependency.

2   When success is defined by an end product, an outcome, or some final achievement, then life tends to be a continuous struggling and striving to 'get there'. Our happiness is continuously delayed. In other words, not such a joy filled journey!

3   If success is defined by the acquisition or accumulation of anything' then fear will always be lurking in the background. Fear of failure' which is the same as the fear of loss. Stress will be your companion.

No matter which way you look at it, success is a personal issue. Like other aspects of how to create a happy and fulfilled life, success tends to be shrouded in many illusions and delusions, depending on our upbringing. Its achievement is now championed by hundreds of success gurus and coaches, mentors and trainers, all waiting in the wings to advise and guide us. Many promising a 'magic formula" which can range from the secrets of attraction to the power of self-belief, from the work harder ethic to the development of your creative genius, from how to 'unleash' your potential to invoking the angels of success to guide your entire life!

But before we listen to anyone (including this article) it's probably worthwhile finding a tree, on a quiet and sunny hillside, by a peaceful meadow, next to meandering river, to sit and gently reflect on what only your own heart can tell you in response to the question, "What does success really mean to me"?

It will of course generate many other questions. Like what is the purpose of my life? What do I value? But then 'they' do say that when it comes to this unique and special journey called life there is a time when asking the 'right questions' is much more important than having the right answers.

Question:
What does success mean to you?

Reflection:
Why do you think your definition of success
might be challenging to achieve?

Action:
Initiate a conversation sometime this week with friends, family
or colleagues, and ask them what success means to them.

Do YOU Suffer From the Dis-ease Called HOPE?

Once upon a time there was a little baby bear that lived in the woods. One day, while out playing, he ran into two badgers. He wanted to play with the badgers but they didn't want to play with him. They wanted to fight. And they did. They bullied the little bear every day for a week. Then, one day, the badgers stopped coming. The baby bear never saw another badger for the rest of his life.

That little baby bear grew up and eventually had his own little baby bear. And the first thing he taught his own baby bear was how evil, wicked and violent badgers were. Little baby bear learned to be fearful of badgers and he hoped he would never ever meet one. Even daddy bear, remembering his fights with the badgers when he was little, would say, "I hope you never meet a badger, those scoundrels, those horrible creatures, I'll never forget them".

For years, as baby bear grew up and roamed the forest, at least once a day he would have the thought, "I hope I don't ever meet a badger, I hope I have a badger free day today!" And as much as he 'thought hopefully' so he feared the badger. Then, one fateful day, he encountered three badgers. They came suddenly out of the bushes laughing and joking with each other. The bear stopped in his tracks, paralyzed by the sight of the badgers. His one and only thought was

"Oh no! BADGERS!" The moment the badgers saw the bear they stopped laughing. They also stood absolutely still as if paralyzed. Then, howling in fear, they scampered back into the bushes.

Now the bear was surprised at this. But it only took a few moments to realize why. He was in fact now five times bigger than the badgers. He was a giant in the badger's eyes. From that day on he never feared badgers again. He never again 'hoped' he would not meet a badger.

And the moral of the story? To live in hope is to live in fear. Hope is often just an attempt to put a positive spin on worry! An oxymoron if ever there was one!

Living in Hope

HOPING for something to happen is also a great way to avoid DOING something to 'make' things happen. Leading sports people, business people, career people, family-raising people, don't sit around hoping for the best, they get up and create the best. They make the best happen because they know they can. That's probably the key phrase; *know they can.* Could that be why so many decide hope is enough? They live in hope because they don't yet KNOW that they can? At best they have learned to habitually doubt themselves and, at worst, they have learned to believe that they can't!

"Hope says that one day I MAY be able. But as long as we just 'live in hope' it's unlikely that day will come."

The bear had learned to believe badgers were bigger and stronger so the foundation of his hope was ignorance. And ignorance begets fear. As soon as he realized he was much bigger, stronger, greater, then hope became irrelevant. Why, because the bears ignorance was dispelled.

Hope says that one day I MAY be able. But as long as we just 'live in hope' it's unlikely that day will ever come. And if it does it's likely to be too late! Somewhere in between are those who are not sure if they can, but they are not prepared to take the risk (fear) to either find out if they can or begin learning 'how to' become able. Perhaps we have all known that state at some time.

Hoping for something better than now!

Why do we live in hope? Why do we think and say that we have high hopes? Why do we hope for a brighter future? Because we don't like the way people are and/or the way circumstances are, right now. We are afraid that the way people/circumstances are now may continue. We are in a 'state of resistance' to the circumstances that we find our self in today. So we hope for a better tomorrow. But hope makes us lazy. It's easier to hope than actually do something now that may create the tomorrow that we say we want. So hope becomes a comfort zone that is easy to slip into. Only our own actions can create a way out, a way beyond hope, a way beyond the paralyzing effect of fear that always underlies hoping.

Either that or we can learn to simply accept the way things are right now, not in helpless surrender, but from the wisdom that reminds us that only acceptance of the way things are in the present is the 'first step' in invoking and influencing change for and in the future. Otherwise we just spend time and energy in resistance to 'now'!

Hoping something bad won't happen in the future

Otherwise known as worry! Worry is simply the fear of losing something in the future that we are comfortable with (i.e. attached to) now. We create an imagined future in which that comfort is lost. For this mental process we have plenty of raw material from which to shape ideas and images of our imagined catastrophes. Thereby frightening our self into a paralysis that prevents action. Much of that material comes from our news and entertainment industries. They are always on hand to feed us with the latest dark events and a pessimistic outlook.

Hoping we will get what we want...eventually!

Just as hoping that something bad won't happen is really fear disguised as hope, so waiting to get exactly what we want is usually desire masquerading as hope. However it's not easy to see that all desire is just a way of delaying our happiness! This comes from the belief that it's only when we get what we want that we can be truly happy. Hoping means that at best we are living for tomorrow today, which is not really living but more like avoiding life. At worst we are trying to live in the future, which is insane, because it's impossible.

So are there ever moments when hope has a place, a value, in life. Are there ever times when hope adds strength? Sometimes we hear or read real life stories of those stranded in impossible and apparently hopeless situations. Perhaps waiting to be rescued at sea or on a mountain. Then they often say, "It was hope that kept us alive". But in such situations hope is usually that absolutely final thought that arises after all other possibilities of escape or survival have been exhausted. It momentarily fends off feelings of helplessness.

It reminds us all to ask the question whenever we find our self saying or even thinking, "I hope...", have we truly exhausted all possible ways to move forward? Have we explored all possible perspectives and perceptions that may allow us to find a different meaning, perhaps ignite the spark of creativity and stir within us the inspiration to take new action?

High Hopes for You

Then there are those moments when we say to the other, "I have high hopes for you'. It sounds eminently positive and yet, when decoded, it usually means high expectations, which usually means desire. We witness this each year in the arena of sport when we have collective 'high hopes' for our sporting heroes. And when they don't live up to our hopes we find ourselves suffering emotionally. Our hopes are dashed by their failure, which means we are living vicariously and once again missing our own life!

Giving Up

Helplessness is the feeling that arises from the belief that the situation is not going to get any better, more than likely it will get much worse and there is nothing we can do to affect change. "It's hopeless", is often what we think, feel and say when we describe our self at our 'wits end'. It's the moment we decide to 'give up' on our self or on the other or on the situation.

"To free your self from feelings of hopelessness is to free your self from your dependency on others or the world for your sense of wellbeing."

Sometimes these thoughts and feelings are entirely appropriate. They are not a sign of a spiral downwards, but a liberation from futility and an acceptance of the reality of the situation. This is usually when giving up really means 'letting go' in relation to an aspect of the situation or relationship e.g. "It was hopeless so I gave up trying to convince them or make them do what I wanted" or "It was a hopeless endeavor so I let go of the idea of making a million by the end of next month". In such contexts while there may be a sense of loss, it's outweighed by a sense of freedom from a self imposed pressure and a kind of helpless hopefulness!

In the Depths of Hopelessness

But many people do experience a deep and mysterious hopelessness, not in specific situations, but just in relation to life and living in general. It can be one of the main symptoms of depression. In such instances it is signaling an absence of wellbeing, it's a feeling of heaviness accompanied by a complete lack of enthusiasm for anything. Described by many as staring into a dark abyss, it's as if there is a huge gaping hole in the soul.

However like all forms of suffering it is a signal something needs to change, not within the world, but within the self. That something is 'always' to do with self-awareness or self-understanding. To free your self from deep feelings of hopelessness is to free your self from our dependency on others or the world for our sense of wellbeing.

Being well starts not with others behaviors, or with our bodies but with our mind and heart. Not the heart of our body but the heart of our being. Feelings of hopelessness arise because we lose sight of the unlimited creative power that we have and that we are...on the inside. We become ignorant of the extraordinary beauty that we have and that we are... on the inside. We have lost the awareness that we are the masters of our own destiny.

Being Bigger

So the opposite of hopelessness, or the cure for hopelessness, is not hope but the realization we are free spirits, tied to nothing and no one, dependent on nothing and no one; that we are not only able to create our own destiny but, in truth, it's what we are here to do. The moment we start to translate that realization into action, hopelessness starts to fade, and hope is known for what it is, a false sense of strength.

The ultimate cure for hopelessness is the realization that nothing can overwhelm us. There is nothing that we cannot face and deal with, nothing that we cannot do if we are prepared to learn or even just try. It's the realization that we are not the baby bear (small and overwhelmed), but the fully-grown bear that is much bigger than all the badgers in the forest. We are all bigger than any situation or circumstance that we have to face. Hence the ancient wisdom in the saying, "You will never be asked by life to face anything that you do not have the capacity to handle". It's just that sometimes our capacity is, as yet, unrealized and life throws us the opportunity to discover it.

So hope and hopelessness are both dis-eases of consciousness. They are symptoms of deeper underlying dis-ease known as ignorance, an ignorance of our self and our innate capacity to live life peacefully, creatively and joyfully. They are signs that we are living in an 'unrealized state' i.e. we don't know how powerful we are...yet!

Feelings of hopefulness and hopelessness are both saying. "It's time to become more self aware". Wake up to your capacity, your power, your ability to deal with anything life can throw at you. With the guidance of someone who already knows the inner territory it's possible to induce the insights and self-knowledge that restores your inner strength to your spiritual muscles!

Then hope is known and used for what it is, a temporary relief from hopelessness. Then it can be a platform from which to spring forth into action, into life.

But don't get stuck standing on the platform!

Question:
What do you hope for your self,
for others and for the world?

Reflection:
Why do you hope what you hope?

Action:
What can you DO that will free you from needing to be
hopeful or from any sense of hopelessness?

Being Balanced or Being Centered What's the Difference?

Do you feel you are living a balanced life? Do you believe you have your priorities right? Is your work interfering with your life or is your life interfering with your work? During this last decade in particular much has been said and written, many courses devised and delivered, on how to achieve that apparently elusive ideal known as the work/life balance.

Some believe they are being forced to work too much at the cost of their relationships with family and friends, while others consciously sacrifice almost all their relationships in favor of work work work! Many are driven by ambition, sometimes as a defense against insecurity, sometimes as a way of avoiding certain 'other issues' in their life. But it may be months or years before they realize they are exhausting themselves in pursuit of something they can never achieve solely through action i.e. self-fulfillment and a happy life.

Then there are those who have little ambition in the world of work but who learn to live with a quiet sense of guilt or a feeling of inadequacy while surrounded by workaholics and ambition addicts. "There must be something wrong with me", they think. Until one day, as they watch the rushaholics and the action addicts burn out, they realize, "There might be something right with me"!

There are some amongst us for whom work is considered to be a 'necessary evil' to be grimly tolerated throughout the average day. Sometimes referred to as a 'wage slave' they seek only the means to pay the mortgage, fill the fridge, sustain the family and feed the dog. They see 'work' as a totally separate 'segment' of their life. They have given up on anything called a career, if they ever got started, and only 'do work' because they feel they 'have to'. They will live almost one third of their life reluctantly, wondering why they are not that happy within the other two thirds, without quite making the connection that you cannot be two people.

Then there are those who are constantly, frenetically, almost obsessively, seeking that magic, utopian work/life balance. A life where time and energy is neatly divided up and spent economically, efficiently and effectively. Conscientious and sensible, they will occasionally explode in frustration unable to face the fact that utopia is not a time management exercise, that the ideal life is not the perfect balance of one's priorities nor the ability to achieve a set of goals on time.

Dropping Pennies

Then there is that very rare individual for whom the penny has dropped on this life/work balance thing! They have realized there is no such thing. They wear a quiet smile when others speak about being stretched all the time, about being so uncontrollably busy, about needing to prioritize better, about being overcome by competing demands, about being stressed by looming deadlines. All these 'symptoms of the unbalanced' are history for the one who has 'cottoned on' to the fact that not only is attempting to achieve a work/life balance futile, it's like all attempts to find perfect balance in life, impossible! They know what few have probably yet to realize, that balance is irrelevant when you become 'centered'!

Attempting to be more balanced is a recipe for tension and anxiety. Watch the tightrope walker and you can see two areas of tension - under his feet and between the two hands holding the long pole. Similarly in life, trying to work out what areas of your life should get your attention without tension, so that other areas are not neglected, can be a continuous source of anxiety and tension! Usually accompanied by the constantly nagging thoughts like, "Am I getting this right? I'm sure I am neglecting something or someone. I just don't know if I have enough time to meet the demands of everything and everyone."

"They know what few have probably yet to realize, that balance is irrelevant when you become 'centered'!"

So what is the difference between the 'balance seeking person' and the 'centered person' for whom the idea of balance has become redundant?

BSP versus CP!

The balance seeking person (BSP) tends to see their life as divided into different segments as they compartmentalize work, family, leisure, education, self-development etc. The centered person (CP) sees their life as a whole, without divisions or compartments. The BSP is frequently trying to measure and calculate the time/attention they give to each segment so there may be a 'fair and balanced sharing'. Whereas the CP gives time and attention according to the needs of the situation and circumstances, knowing there are always ebbs and flows and that ultimately any and all extremes settle back into the 'center'. They average out naturally.

Guilty Feelings

The BSP will tend to generate guilt when they start to think they are not giving adequate time and attention to some area of their life or particular relationships in their life. Whereas the CP never feels guilty about how they spend their time, as they never see themselves wasting time or losing time. They know that they bring 'value' to whatever or wherever they choose to focus their attention.

The balance seeking person (BSP) spends almost as much time worrying about what others will think of them if they don't attend to their needs and priorities. Whereas the centered person (CP) never worries about what other people think about how they use their time i.e. live their life! Even if they are judged by others it doesn't bother them. They are free spirits and their centeredness is unshakable.

Give or Get

The fundamental difference between a balance seeking person (BSP) and a centered person (CP) is one of 'intention'. The BSP's intention is mostly to 'get something from', whereas the CPs intention is to 'give something to'. Although the BSP believes they are giving time and attention to each segment of their life, their underlying motive is to get something from each area. They see each area of their life as a source of something that they believe they have to 'acquire' e.g. work means get the money, family means get love and happiness, leisure time means get some relaxation and pleasure, education means getting knowledge.

On the other hand the CP's intention is to 'give something to' because they don't see themselves as needy. They see themselves as a source of energy in their life and they are available to give whatever is needed to whomever and whenever it is possible. And if they can't, then they can't! The 'energy' that they do give can take one of many forms e.g. time, attention, ideas, wisdom, support, caring, finance, advice etc. The BCP tends to be rigid in whatever contribution they do make whereas the CP tends to be flexible and is both able and willing to give what is needed.

Expectation to be Met

This means the BSP has expectations within each area of their life and therefore the anxiety that those expectations will not be met and anger when they are often not fulfilled. Whereas the CP has no expectations and if they do, they remain centered, as their happiness is not dependent on having any expectations met.

The BSP hasn't quite realized that wanting and taking are precursors to fear and frustration and are therefore disempowering. Whereas the CP knows that giving and sharing are the foundation of self-empowerment and self-fulfillment. Not an easy connection to make if one has been conditioned by a culture that celebrates getting what you want before someone else does. It is the difference between these two mindsets that allows the CP to remain consistently content regardless of what is happening in any area of their life.

"While our 'innate values' can never be lost or stolen, our 'acquired values' are vulnerable to removal."

Meaning of Life

The deepest difference between the 'balance seeker' and 'the centered' is around the meaning they ascribe to life itself. For the BSP life will often be seen as a burden, an obstacle course, a struggle to get through, something to be managed and survived. Whereas the CP is more likely to see life as a gift, as an opportunity to be creative, co-creative with others, and a playful adventure.

The BSP will likely live their life shaped by a set of acquired values, imposed by others, around material things like possessions, position, and financial security. Whereas the CP will live according to their 'realized' innate values such as love and caring, compassion and joy. Hence their ability to remain stable when everyone else is in chaos. While one's 'innate values' can never be lost or stolen, 'acquired values' are vulnerable to removal; hence the BSP's frequent anxiety about what is going to happen next!

While the BSP will seek some kind of recognition and approval to affirm their worth in each segment of their life, the CP does not seek attention or approval in any area or from anyone. Their self-worth and self-esteem are self-generated from within their 'center'.

The BSP lives from outside in, whereas the CP lives from inside out. And while the BSP is frequently looking for tools and techniques to be more balanced in their life, the CP knows there are no techniques to living from the center. They know that only the cultivation of self-awareness and a clear intellect are required to make the choices and decisions that ensure time and energy flows outwards naturally 'from' their center.

While the BSP may seek a life coach to help them find balance in their values, goals, priorities and time allocations, the CP knows that eventually they will become their own coach. They have realized that living a fulfilling and happy life is not something that can be forced or shaped by others or the world, it has to come from the heart.

For that is where the center lies. Not the heart of the body, but the heart of the being. And there is only one coach who awaits us there!

Question:
Why do so many feel that their life is out of balance?

Reflection:
According to your awareness of the attributes of a centered
person, which ones are strong and which
ones are weak within you?

Action:
Take five minutes at the end of each day this weak, review the day, and find
moments when you felt out of balance and
moments when you were centered.

And Finally...Time for a Laugh?

Taking something apart, like a watch or a television, in order to find out how it works is usually a self-defeating exercise. The moment they are broken into their component parts they stop working! Humor and comedy are almost the same. Analyzing why we laugh brings laughter to an end. Trying to separate out what makes comedy comically funny kills humor. Therefore reflecting on what may be the magic ingredients that have the power to induce hilarity is probably a futile exercise. But lets do it anyway!

We now know for sure that hearty laughter stimulates beneficial, even life preserving chemicals in the body. The short-term effects can be dramatic; tension is dispersed, apprehension is banished, our ability to think positively is increased, and contentment is restored. In the longer term there is a case to be made for some deep, 'from the belly', laughter every day. The now famous Patch Adams became known for his work with sick children, recognizing their laughter as the essential component in their return to good health. He would literally get into bed with the chronically depressed and teach them how to laugh. Then there was Norman Cousins, diagnosed with an incurable disease, who found the anesthetic effect of ten minutes laughter dissolved his pain for two hours. He checked out of hospital and into a hotel room where, for two weeks, he laughed at comedy videos all day. Eventually cured, he spent the rest of his life teaching the medical benefits of laughter.

Laughter Clubs

Some scientists have been busy studying mirth and hilarity for some time! According to scientific journals over the past few decades the efficacy of a good laugh is unchallengeable as it reduces cortisol and increases endorphins – the bodies natural opiates that make us happy; it eases muscle tension; it increases the bodies T Cell count; it aids ventilation; it increases flow of oxygen and nutrients to the tissues; it increases 'catecholanes' which boost mental alertness and reduces the rate of cellular decay.

"There is a case to be made for some deep, 'from the belly', laughter every day."

Laughter can also shift our perception allowing us to view problems in an entirely different light. No surprise then that there are laughter clubs across the world where people start their day with 45 minutes of group laughter. Apparently they begin with a simple ha ha...hee hee...ho ho (try saying it out loud now!) and work up from there into an infectious, collective wave of continuous audible glee!

One of the enduring roles within every society is the comic. The evolution from the court jester playing to a privileged few to the comic playing to thousands on flood lit stages across the world means the modern comedian has the power to fill auditoriums and have an audience both on their feet and at their feet. Their ability to induce uproarious laughter, especially around what are considered 'dark' topics, in darkened halls, in what can appear to be darkening times, is a highly prized talent.

Despite 24-hour comedy channels on TV, many of us are still prepared to pay 'top dollar' for this kind of entertainment, which can border on mass therapy. Why, because the comic's role is to temporarily dissolve our anxieties. They are agents of release and relaxation. They puncture the tension of our pretensions, allowing a rush of fresh air into our consciousness. They can induce our laughter despite ourselves. The comic spirit breaks down inner barriers, working against the forces of gravitas, undermining our resistance to delight.

Types of Laughter

But our laughter in life does not always come sunny side up. There is even a shadow side to humor, perversions of delight that are not wholly healthy. A list of modern reasons to be cheerful reveals many different forms of laughter. There is the laughter of the *cruel* as we celebrate the suffering of another. There is the laughter of *derision* as we scoff at another's failure or inadequacy. There is the laughter of *high spirits*, a kind of childlike and over stimulated excitement. There is the laughter of *nervousness* when we try to disguise our fears. There is the laughter of *relief*, when a deeply felt tension or pain is finally dissolved. There is the laughter of *bravado* as we celebrate our courage at breaking some rule or cultural taboo. There is the laughter of *self-consciousness* as we try to disguise our discomfort at being the focus of attention. And there is the laughter of *manipulation* in which we force our self to laugh at another's humor in order to preserve their approval of us, and perhaps gain more favor.

"Apparently they begin with a simple ha ha...hee hee...ho ho (try saying it out loud now!) and work up from there into an infectious, collective wave of continuous audible glee."

Involuntary laughter

While these forms of laughter may not be the best reasons to be cheerful they serve to confirm the purity and the priceless value of genuine wit. And while 'wittiness' appears to becoming increasingly impromptu, the well rehearsed joke that moves from premise to punch line, is still the genre that reigns supreme at 'comedy HQ'! Jokes, like myths, serve a purpose in society. To tell one, especially to a group, is to assume an important mantle – that of the storyteller - breaking down inhibitions and uniting an audience in a shared involuntary response. Not only do we laugh from our heart, we might also notice the comic's unseen role is to unite a thousand hearts with humor. As we laugh with others we look around and for a split second the hearts of strangers melt together. We are briefly as one, united by mirth and the mirth maker.

"Despite 24-hour comedy channels on TV, many of us are still prepared to pay 'top dollar' for this kind of entertainment, which can border on mass therapy."

This reminds us of what some see as the real meaning of 'humor'? 'Hu' is an ancient chant for God while 'mour' is somehow connected to 'amour' or love. So pure humor is likened to a divine energy that does what pure love does, it creates unity and harmony both within us and between us. Perhaps the closest we can get to pure laughter, pure humor, is the innocent joy of the child who has not yet learned to believe that the world might be a seriously dangerous place. In a world where we can easily find a thousand reasons to be miserable perhaps the real comic we all need to discover is our 'inner comic'.

An ability self-reflect and to laugh at ones self is, for some people, not an easy thing to do. While children will readily laugh at themselves, adults tend to be wary that self-mockery might be seen to undermine their commitment to 'grown up' responsibility. In fact, being unable to laugh at ourselves may indicate that we find it hard to recognize our own foibles. We then become susceptible to pomposity, pride, vanity and the like.

Perhaps this is why one particular definition of comedy rings true. It's been said that 'comedy is tragedy plus time'. Which feels right if only because our ability to laugh at our self requires a time lapse in which we can reflect on an absurd mistake or a clumsy action which, at the time, seemed far from funny.

One thing is for sure; everyone has a different view of what is funny. What tickles one person is simply bizarre to another. In some cultures slapstick is the greatest cause for hilarity, in others it's just corny. For some people with a rigid national or cultural conditioning just being alive is such a serious business that laughter is almost seen as treating life with contempt. Other, perhaps more enlightened communities, see life itself is a divine comedy, a cosmic joke, and if you take it seriously you do so at your peril!

It does seem however that the staple amusement of almost all cultures is still the 'joke' served up as a very short story involving characters we can in some way, however tenuously, identify with.

The World's Favorite Joke

Some time ago The LaughLab set out to find the world's favorite joke. And so in the interest of your good health and to give you the opportunity to share the gift of YOUR laughter with whoever may be in the same room as you read this, here is the joke that got the most votes.

Sherlock Holmes and Dr Watson were on a camping trip. They pitched their tent under the stars and went to sleep. Sometime in the middle of the night Holmes woke Watson up and said: "Watson, look up at the stars, and tell me what you see." Watson replied: "I see millions and millions of stars." Holmes said: "and what do you deduce from that?"

Watson replied: "Well, if there are millions of stars, and if even a few of those have planets, it's quite likely there are some planets like earth out there. And if there are a few planets like earth out there, there might also be life." And Holmes said: "Watson, you idiot, it means that somebody stole our tent."

I must confess, while I did laugh at this the one that tickled me the most was this. Something close to what used to be called a 'shaggy dog story'.

An Alsatian went to a telegram office, took out a blank form and wrote: "Woof. Woof. Woof. Woof. Woof. Woof. Woof. Woof. Woof." The clerk examined the paper and politely told the dog: "There are only nine words here. You could send another 'Woof' for the same price."

"But," the dog replied, "That would make no sense at all."

Which perhaps confirms that when it comes to humor there is, as they say, no accounting for taste!

Question:
What in life do you take most seriously and that is the hardest thing to raise even a smile about ... and why?

Reflection:
How would you categorize the most common reason for your laughter – comedy, absurdity, cruelty, derision, nervousness, relief, bravado, self-consciousness, manipulation?

Action:
During the coming week consciously lighten up a different relationship with your laughter each day.

Thanks and Links

Thanks to some of the most powerful and beautiful retreat centers where you can find the space 'to be' and the clarity 'to see,' during many kinds of weekend retreats!

UK: www.globalretreatcentre.com
USA: (East Coast) www.peacevillageretreat.org
(West Coast) www.anubhutiretreatcenter.org
Australia: www.brahmakumaris.org/au/spiritual-retreats
Italy: www.casasangam.org
India: www.omshantiretreat.org; www.shantisarovar.org

Thanks to **Lucinda** and **Andy** for the kind of music that seeps into your heart and nourishes the soul.
www.blissfulmusic.com

Thanks to Marneta and **Relax Kids** for showing us all how to reach the hearts of the children of the world.
www.relaxkids.com

Thanks to the **BKs**, where anyone can receive free tuition in meditation and begin anything from a simple meditation practice to a personal spiritual journey in centers in over 100 countries.
www.bkwsu.org

Gratitude to the **Ammerdown Retreat Centre** – an oasis of calm and tranquility in which to gather for an intimate retreat, as we do in August every year.
www.ammerdown.org

Deep appreciation to **Cotrugli Business School**, the progressive business school that serves the Balkans and makes learning and unlearning fun and enlightening.
www.cotrugli.eu

Deep appreciation for all the work of friends at **Comic Relief** as they carry both our cash and our compassion into a world of deprivation and violence that is the fate of so many children.
www.comicrelief.com

And finally, congratulations and gratitude to **Piero Musini** for creating 'Santa Pasta,' the new king of pastas – the healthiest, the tastiest, and made with the most elevated energies in the most organic way!
www.santapasta.it

About the Author

Mike George 'plays' a variety of roles including author, spiritual teacher, coach, management tutor, mentor and facilitator. He brings together the three key strands of 21st century - emotional/spiritual intelligence, leadership development and continuous 'unlearning.'

In a unique blend of insight, wisdom and humor Mike entertains as he enlightens, speaks to your heart as he stay's out of your head and points to 'the way' as he waves you off on your journey!

Some of his previous books include: *BEING Your Self; The 7 Myths About LOVE... Actually!; The Immune System of the SOUL; Don't Get MAD Get Wise; The 7 AHA!s of Highly Enlightened Souls; In the Light of Meditation; Learn to Find Inner Peace; Learn to Relax.*

Each year he leads awareness and enlightenment retreats across the world including Africa, Australia, Argentina, Brazil, Chile, Croatia, Germany, Italy, Mexico, Scandinavia, Spain and throughout the UK and USA

Mike can be contacted at **mike@relax7.com** and a schedule of his seminars and talks can usually be found at **www.relax7.com**

If you would like to receive Mike's regular e-article entitled **Clear Thinking** you can subscribe at www.relax7.com - it's free.

For more of Mike's insights, workshops, retreats, seminars, talks, articles and meditations see:

www.relax7.com
www.mythsoflove.com
www.mikegeorgebooks.com

Lightning Source UK Ltd.
Milton Keynes UK
UKOW06f2013091017

310682UK00005B/194/P